UNEXPECTED TURBULENCE

WHEN LIFE SUDDENLY BECOMES UNIDENTIFIABLE AND YOU REALIZE THAT YOU ARE NOT IN COMPLETE CONTROL OVER YOUR PLANS OR YOUR DESTINY.

Dr. T.R. Anderson

ISBN 978-1-64079-310-1 (Paperback)
ISBN 978-1-64079-311-8 (Digital)

Copyright © 2017 by Dr. T.R. Anderson
All rights reserved. No part of this publication may be reproduced, distributed, or transmitted in any form or by any means, including photocopying, recording, or other electronic or mechanical methods without the prior written permission of the publisher. For permission requests, solicit the publisher via the address below.

Christian Faith Publishing, Inc.
296 Chestnut Street
Meadville, PA 16335
www.christianfaithpublishing.com

Printed in the United States of America

Contents

Preface 1
Acknowledgments 5
Love Letter 9
Introduction 11
Turbulence 15
Grief Can't Be Fixed 21
Forgiving God (Meet James) 31
"If Only" (Meet Barbara) 53
Freewill vs God's Will (Meet Amanda) 71
Why Did This Happen To Us (Meet Teena) 83
Where Were You God? (Meet Nick and Nina) 91
Finding Peace 117
Conclusion What's Left Over 123

PREFACE

*J*ust keep moving; you will survive the experience of a death. When we lose someone, we are in a dichotomy of making sense out of living, after the experience of death. Basically, death has obstructed our way of living, and our ability to carry on with day-to-day task.

While on this journey of writing this book, I had the pleasure of meeting a gentle spirit who I will only introduce as Ms. T. I met Ms. T at a function at my church where she was introduced to the audience and asked to bless us with her gift, and with the most gentleness, grace, and elegance, she declined. Instead, Ms. T grabbed the microphone and thanked the group for their support and prayers during what she referred to as a "rough time." She spoke with confidence that was embodied in sincere appreciation, and I was drawn in, and even though I wasn't sure what she was thanking the group for, nor what they had prayed about, she was infectious. Ms. T may have been experiencing a dark state, but her spirit illuminate the room, and whatever she was experiencing, I knew she was going to get through it; she reeked of hope and perseverance. I wanted to meet her, I needed to meet her, I needed her to talk some more.

When Ms. T was leaving the event, I paid her a simple compliment about her hair, and just as she had done in the room with the microphone, she began to speak in a gentleness that resembled a "seasoned kind spirit." She was no amateur at kindness, she had poured into many, many spirits during her lifetime, and now it was my turn. Ms. T shared with me that she had experienced the death of her husband after being married for over fifty-three years and she was now alone. She said it had been less than six months since he passed away and she was feeling the awkwardness of being alone, without her companion, without her best friend. This was an event that they had attended many times together, and now Ms. T was faced with a change in her social status.

When she spoke, I noticed her subtle pauses, and how she spoke every word carefully, as if she was almost singing a soft melody of the experience. In that moment, I had what Oprah Winfrey refers to as an "aha moment," which changed and challenged my thinking about additional aspects of loss and survival that I had not considered. Ms. T had spent a half of a century with her husband and losing him and his companionship created an abundance of shifting newness, including how she spoke. Ms. T had been speaking the love language of "we and us" for over fifty years, and on this particular day, Ms. T was on a journey of learning how to speak in a singular vernacular of "me and I" and even in that challenge of change, I still felt the hope. The hope of what the future holds for Ms. T in her new uninvited singleness and her journey of change. Ms. T also shared that she had not participated in any social events since her husband's death and that she had toiled with not going to the event where I met her. She said she had changed her mind several times, but she kept getting a strong push from her husband's memory and she knew that he would want her to attend. I told her that it was not by chance that she and I had met and shared with her that I was in the process of writing this book and I was drawn to her and her "rough time." I told her that there were several keys to healing an experience of sudden death, and I recommended that she start with committing to "just keep moving, and trust God's plan for life her." I also warned her to pay close attention to her daily routines, as it can offer complacency that could render her in a rut, with a sense of hopelessness about being left behind.

When you feel hopeless about your situation or your future, it can also lead to depression or other mental and physical illnesses. What your mind tries to deny, your body will absorb and tell you when it is under attack or being strained. It's important to pay attention to how you care for your day and yourself. Each of us have or will experience sadness, pain, and some level of depression in our lives as a result of death. The most important of your daily task is to make sure that you talk to God every day, put your hope in Him and his word and his promises, pray, and read his word. God will extend you "new" grace to deal with the new day, every day. He warns us not to worry, when he tells us, "Therefore do not worry about tomorrow, for tomorrow will worry about itself. Each day has enough trouble of its own" (*Matthew 6:34*).

Most people question God when they are in a storm or trail, they wonder how God could allow such hurt and devastation on earth, how could he not intervene in tragic situations, especially mine, after all, I've been a good person. Then there are some who question whether they deserve the experience that they are having, because of their past partakes or mistakes. God is not shocked when we question him or our experience; in fact, I believe God expects us to ask him why, even Jesus asked God, why he had forsaken him, while he was on the cross-suffering persecution for a sin fluid world. I suggest if you question God, or should I say, when you question God, also ask him to reveal His will for your life and remember to trust his answer and his promises, be patient, when you are ready, he will give all the answers you can handle. Ask Him to reveal to you his plan for your new life, cry out to the God, "What's next for me, Lord?" Just don't lose heart, keep the faith, he will show and lead you on your unfamiliar path.

I told Ms. T never lose her hope, to accept every invitation to participate in social events, including staying connected to her local church, family, friends—all these things require that you "keep moving" God will help you with the rest.

Acknowledgments

I want to first and foremost thank God for creating a space for me to finish this project, and as always, for keeping his promises of never forsaking those who love him and are called according to his purpose, thank you, Lord! I also want to thank those people who are part of this project and decided to live even after the heartbreaking experience of a death. Your courage and perseverance is a visual witness of God's grace and mercy, even during the most tragic of circumstance. Thank you for sharing and trusting me with your pain, tears, and uncertainties. I am forever changed.

I want to also thank my family and friends who showed me unconditional love when I was experiencing my own unexpected turbulence. Many of you made room for me and my storm in your lives and gave me some encouraging words, a text message of hope, a helping hand, a prayer, a place to just be quiet, a place to cry, or a place to laugh until I cried. There are just too many of you to name without risking leaving someone out, but I want the reader to know that I was surrounded by love, which gave me the opportunity to focus on the peace that God gives while you're in an unfair brawl with principalities. No one but God could win such a fight, or should I say, no one without God will ever be prepared for the fight. The odds are against you, it's an unfair fight, and just as Joseph said in his posture of reconcile and forgiveness of his brothers after they betrayed him, "You intended to harm me, but God intended it for good to accomplish what is now being done, the saving of many lives" (*Genesis 50:20, NIV*). It is this author's belief that "you have not truly lived until you have experienced death." Sometimes it's your own death, the death of your "old self" that might thrust you into mourning. So when life became unrecognizable and filled with uncertainty for me, I was grateful to have so many people show me love, thank you, Lord, for my village.

I am not suggesting that any of this is an easy street to be on; we all know the unknown is an uncomfortable place, and we wonder what the future will look like. However, what I am suggesting is, life is filled with swift transitions, and at some point, you will experience some unexpected turbulence that could render you unconscious of your normal existence, and your old way of living and thinking will no longer be accessible. Just the thought of it is frightening, but the experience of it is horrific, and those of us who have already experienced some life turbulence, in unison, we say, get ready for all the things that may come your way in this unknown state of being. You might ask, how does one get ready and prepare for an "unfair flight"? This author's answer is, you have to equip your mind, body, and soul by spending time with God (though prayer), ask him for what you need (through reading), read God's word, he will tell you what to do, and (through fellowship), join a Bible-based church, and attend regularly. God will not only send you some visual help, while he stands in the ring for you, and take control of the invisible brawl with principalities, but He can also resurrect you with the living and guide you in your newness, to live in his will. You will have to trust in God, and His promises, *"For I know the plans I have for you," declares the* LORD, *"plans to prosper you and not to harm you, plans to give you hope and a future"* (Jeremiah 29:11, NIV). I was encouraged by Paul's example, when he said in Philippians 3:13–14, *"Brothers and sisters, I do not consider myself yet to have taken hold of it. But one thing I do: Forgetting what is behind and straining toward what is ahead, I press on toward the goal to win the prize for which God has called me heavenward in Christ Jesus."* This is a temporary life; we are all going to leave here, focus on your heaven-bound journey, put your hope in God, and never give up! Know that suffering will introduce you to the stronger side of your existence.

LOVE LETTER

Hello, my dearest loved one,

I know you are surprised to hear from me. I know how much you must miss me in the physical. I know you think about me at almost every occasion and gathering that I am absent. I know how difficult it was for you to lose me and how you feel that I left too soon. I can't even imagine if it were the other way around and you had left me here to continue on without you. I can only imagine how many times you have cried and how much your heart aches over losing me. I know you think you could have done something that would have changed the outcome of my passing away. I know you have so many thoughts and questions about my last thoughts, my feelings about dying, and what I left undone. I know you have asked God why and you asked God where he was, and why he didn't intervene on my behalf. I want you to know, he was with me, he made it painless, he made it easy, he made it peaceful, it was everything I ever imagined; in fact, it was wonderful. Which brings me to why I am writing you; it's hard to bask in the pleasure of his company and know that although you are living, you are not at peace, that you still question my leaving, that you are soooo sad at times.

I know if you had left me, you would want me to "*live*" and stay on course with my life, and God's plan for my life; well, I feel the same way. The last thing I want for you is sadness or despair; you and I both know that life only offers us a short time on earth. Feel free to tell me what you wish you could have said to me before I left. I am listening, I hear you, I feel you, but most of all, I see you, and I don't like what I see. It's not uncommon for people to say, "Rest in peace." I assure you, I am trying, but it's hard for me to rest in peace when you seem to be overtaken by sadness and grief because I am not there anymore. I am in agony for you and how you are living without me. I'm stuck between pleasure and pain. God does care about you, and yes, he cared about me; it was a part of the plan, and believe it or not, God still has a plan for you. He can still use you, your pain, your hopes, your dreams; just give him a chance to help you heal, to help you chase your dreams. Keep the faith, you can get through this, he lives in you, he loves you. I'm praying for you and me, I'm praying that you will start to *live* in your newness, without me, and I'm praying that I can begin to "rest in peace."

I love you forever, signed your dearly departed.

INTRODUCTION

Life has a way of presenting us with many unexpectancies throughout the life span. Those times, when we are postured in life's normal predictable routines, whatever they are, times when we are most comfortable with our plight in life, comfortable with our relationships, regardless if it's spouse, children, mother, father, sister, brother, or any relationship, that has slipped into expectancy, the fact is it can be disrupted without warning and everything you thought was in order can become chaotic in seconds. Everything you believed was important can be brought into question, things that needed your immediate attention, that you thought couldn't happen without your involvement will either happen, wait, or become insignificant. Life can be blindsided by the call in the middle of the night, or the persistent knock on the door from the uniformed professional, who just stares at you somberly, or the family member who just shows up at the job and ask you to come with them because there is an emergency, or the doctor's deliberate slow pace down the emergency room hallway as he tries not to look at you or any of your family members head on, or that family member's loud piercing scream that you will never forget in your life; it's those experiences of loss that are at the root of "life's unexpected turbulence." Those times that just show up when things seem to be going good or are in perfect order, that can leave no time to even gasp for air, no time to complete undone task or get back to your life's seat and buckle up for the significant instability in the atmosphere. The unexpected turbulence of loss can cause an emotional event that takes control of your thoughts and actions for an unknown period of time. It is a deliberate, offensive, tormenting of your normal life, creating unnatural amounts of emotional thoughts and pain. It is a time when day and night cross paths, where calm and panic entwine, love and hate share seats, it's the *big one*, the one that either awakes you, assures you, or reminds you, that you are in *control* of *nothing*! I promise, you are not alone. I want to thank all those who shared their stories and experience with me; I am still praying for your deliverance of peace and that your new normal on your life's path is filled with hope, and that you trust God's plan for the future.

For those of you who have currently been blindsided by the experiencing of turbulence, I recommend that you buckle up, as you meet others who have faced similar unexpectancies. People who have been tossed to and from as a result of the loss of their love ones. They show us the cost of loss, the stain and strain of loss, the regrets and the debts of loss, and they show us that no matter how painful and uncomfortable the experience is, even on those days, when we want to just walk right out of this life, that we are left with the task of managing, they show us that we can get through it, if we just keep moving.

I want to share with you that this book is not about how long the grieving process last or when the healing will begin, nor does it offer a guarantee that at the end of the book you will have the answers you need about your experience and pain or what will transpire after you have completed the grieving process. In fact, this author doesn't make any promises at all that things will get better in a certain time frame, and depending on the loss, some of you might experience the similar emotion that those who experience the motion of unexpected turbulence on a plane, it might create uncertainty, fear, and panic all at once and is likely to occur over and over again as days, weeks, and months go by. You will get through it if you trust God, even in your depths of despair and pain. God is the one who sits high and looks low; he is the ever-present help in a time of need, a heart fixer, a bridge over trouble water. You know all the things you have heard about him; now you have to put him to the test. Did I say he was a promise keeper? The only guarantee that this author can offer the reader is "hope"—hope in God and His word on restoration and grief. The how, when, and what the future will look like is unknown, what is known, is "all things, works for the good of those who love him, and are called according to his purpose" (Romans 8:28). God has left us a comforter to help us on the journey of grief. He will have your front, your back, and all your sides if you just trust him to guide you through the untrustworthy emotions of grief. The pain and hurt associated with grief matures us and makes us ready for service, even if we are not willing to serve… "Until you have experienced the death of someone you have truly loved, you have not lived . . . Because you have not lived, you are not ready to die.

TURBULENCE

Turbulence is defined by *Webster* as a great commotion or agitation; irregular atmospheric motion, characterized by up-and-down currents, radical movements or a state of confusion, violence and disorder. Many of us have been introduced to an experience of turbulence while flying on an airplane and for those of us that are frequent flyers, we have had more than our share of in air movement, which is how the title of the book was born, through my own experience of turbulence mid-flight. Turbulence can interrupt the smooth ride of a plane when flying through pockets of rising, falling and rolling air, which has been referred to as eddies. The severity of the turbulence is based on how big the eddies are combined with the strength of the wind shear and the speed of the plane, which could impact how the plane is affected by the turbulence.

My own personal experience with flying caused me to make a promise that I would never fly again. During a flight from Tampa, Florida, to Oakland, California, we experienced a sudden violent shaking on the plane. The plane hit turbulence, causing it to dip and then dropped at least five hundred feet, or that's what I remember. What I also remember is the fear and terror it caused me and others on the flight, which resulted in me making a promise to God; my promise was, "Lord, if you allowed us to land safely, I will never fly again." Needless to say, that has turned out to be another broken promise to God, but for at least seven years, I kept my promise and never got on a plane, but I believe it was more out of fear than being a promise keeper. Since breaking my promise to God, who graciously allowed us to land safely; I have flown more times than I care to count. Even today, I still have apprehensions about flying, but I have learned is, that I control nothing, not even my own destiny. I have also learned to depend on and trust God to guide the way. I admit I still listen for the routine rituals during flights to help guide me through the process. The first bell, we have reached ten thousand feet, it's safe to pull your seat back tray out and let you seat back; you can also use your portable devices. Two bells, flight attendants, "You are able to get up and move about the cabin to start inflight service." What I listen for is the bell that has informed us that the "fasten the seat belt" sign has been turned off and the passengers are free to move about the cabin. Prior to that release of freedom from the seat, I am usually tense, deep in thought, and praying that the Lord has dispatched the angels. The bells are just a part of the routine and offer a false sense of safety during the flight, but they have served as my guide post for the flight; it directs my ability to relax and focus. When I hear the two bells followed by the "fasten your seat belt" sign illuminated mid-flight, then I can usually feel my body become tense again, reacting to the situation. I wait and listen for the announcement that follows the two bells; it's usually a warning from the pilot, "Ladies and gentlemen, please return to your seat, we expect some turbulence and it's going to get a little bumpy ahead," which is usually followed by, "I'll let you know when it's safe to move about the cabin again." Most people, if they are anything like me, are both tense and relieved at the same time: tense because they know the plane will begin to shake, relieved because the pilot knew it was coming and he could adjust the air space if needed and predict when the experience will end.

Much like life, when turbulence is unexpected and offers no warning, even the pilot, is surprised by the violence that causes disruption in the smoothness of the ride; it's those times that give cause for panic, it's those times that alters the sense of security of the passengers and flight attendants, it's those times when everyone is made aware that they lack complete control of the plane or their own destiny and cause's one to question his or her mortality. As for life's unexpected turbulence, it can just show up and bring forth the type of experience that can knock the wind out of you; it's "invisible trouble" that you never saw coming, like an unwelcome, uninvited house guest. The type of unexpectancy that shows up when a perfectly healthy family member suddenly has a heart attack on the subway while riding home, or the plane that's carrying your spouse and children crashes, or the call that came notifying you that your child was shot dead in the streets, or your father that you just hung up the phone with dies for no apparent reason, or the experiences of those families who suffered a loss when the planes intentionally flew into the twin tower buildings on September 11, or the thousands loss during a tsunami, or Hurricane Katrina. Leaving the survivors confused and holding on to the last conversation they had with the departed loved one, having no idea that they would never get another opportunity to say another word to them. Holding on to the last meal they shared, the last hug they gave, or even the last argument that they were involved in. Turbulence that can leave anyone with a heavy heart, where there are no second chances, no matter how good and faithful you have been, no matter how much prayer you have rendered, no matter how long you have served, at some point, death will come knocking on everyone's door and leave you gasping for air, shaken by confusion and questioning God and His plan for your life.

The unexpectancy of the death of someone you love can cause an interruption in your life and your life's daily routines; the routine things we do without thinking, like the route home from work, the drive through for the morning cup of coffee, the "good morning" to the security guard at the front desk of the building we work in, the trip to the mailbox, the closing of the garage door, just normal routine things that we do "by heart" that require no thought, can be difficult to perform, nothing will ever be the same again. The effects of turbulences can be compared to a wheat farmer's harvest season; when he prepares the wheat for market, the farmer violently sifts the wheat to detach from the grain. During biblical times, wheat was connected to the main source of food that required some intense work. The sifting of wheat was done manually, and the process of sifting wheat was to loosen the chaff from the edible grain, which was referred to as threshing and required the wheat to be spread on a floor made of stone or concrete and it was beaten with a flair or whip. The process of sifting wheat was considered one of the most violent actions in produce. God Almighty himself told Simon Peter that he was going to pray that his faith did not fail, because Satan had requested to sift him in the same manner, specifically, *"Simon, Simon, Satan has asked to sift all of you as wheat. [32] But I have prayed for you, Simon, that your faith may not fail. And when you have turned back, strengthen your brothers"* (Luke 22:31–32, NIV), it was clear that Simon's experience was a request from Satan, but it was as God allowed; it served a purpose, it was not only to build Simon's strength, it was to equip or prepare Simon to strengthen others, not if, but when they experienced the same type of vicious turbulence that life brings. Sharing your experience with others can strengthen you and them. God also offered Simon hope in the turbulent storm, not only did he give Simon an unquestionable assignment, he also offered him "hope" that he would get through the turbulence, when he said, "and when you have turned back," meaning that eventually the experience would be behind him. God is praying for us in our storm; he gives us an assignment to share the turbulence we have experienced, or what is better known as a "testimony" so that our experiences can give others a measure of hope. We serve as the physical proof that they can and will get through the turbulence. Faith and hope in God is where we will get the strength to weather the storm, and God is our soft place to land when we fall. Ask God to pray for you, that your "faith may not fail" so that you can be used for the assignment ahead.

Grief Can't Be Fixed

Death and loss is universal and unavoidable, and at some point, each of us will have an experience of loss that can spiral us into a grief experience. Although the experience of grieving may be comparable, one's reaction to loss and the grieving process is unique and no two individuals will grieve the same, even if they have loss the same person. In fact, as much as bereavement is universally painful and complex, it is filled and controlled by the most simplistic emotions common to man, denial, shock, anger, guilt, pain, acceptance, hope, and not in that order and not always identifiable in the experience. It's sad but true; grief can't be fixed. For some people, the process takes longer than others; there is no set length of time or depth of emotion associated with the grieving period nor is there a predetermined reaction to the experience; it is equally common and completely different at the same time, a grief reaction, is personal! Just feel it, let it happen, don't try and control the emotion associated with the stage of or the part of process you find yourself in. Even though it doesn't feel good, there is value in the feelings and there is life after the experience of death.

Grief has been described as a multidimensional emotional reaction to an experience of loss that is usually deeply rooted in a love connection to what is no longer possible. Sigmund Freud (the father of psychoanalysis) explained that grief is a reaction to the loss of a loved person, or some abstraction that has taken the place of one. Many scholars have carefully outlined how grief works and the many stages associated with the grieving process. Because each person has a different reaction to grief, some scholars recommend that grief stages should only be examined as a guide of what to expect when you are going through the grieving process and not a comprehensive explanation of the grief experience.

Let's examine grief from a technological stance for just a minute, the grief process is explained as a series of stages that include, but are not limited to, denial, anger, bargaining, depression, and acceptance, and not necessarily in that order, nor is the process fixed.

DENIAL AND SHOCK

When one experiences a loss through sudden death, the most common immediate reaction to the death is *denial and shock*. Some people have described the experience as being equivalent to having an "out-of-body experience," something peculiar or abnormal. The denial and shock are often responded to with comments like, "It just can't be true, I just hung up the phone with them," or "I just saw them this morning, are you sure?" There are side effects to a grief reaction that is weighted in denial and shock that could leave you questioning everything about the person's life and your very own existences. The side effects, albeit normal, if unattended could lead to major behavior changes, including depression, panic attacks, and anxiety that could affect one's cognitive, physical, spiritual, and social well-being. The loss of a loved one can be saturated with pain, hurt, darkness, and confusion that can penetrate the mind, body, and soul all at once. Frankly, death can be experienced as a cognitive and emotional explosive that is deeply rooted in sorrow and regret, but I assure you that death is as common as living. The experience of loss might feel like it just too much to bear, which could cause one to freeze in motion and render the survivor temporarily unidentifiable even to his or her own self. Most human beings avoid dealing with the reality of here today and gone tomorrow because it is frightening. This avoided fear, which might be responsible for why we take life and close relationships for granted and act as if they are fixed and permanent, until death happens. The sudden disruption of the usual day-to-day busyness of life can leave the survivor fighting to create a new normal, and at times, it might feel like it's just too much to bear. We tend to consider life and death as separate and distinct, but the truth is, life and death are co-heirs to the life cycle; they go together and are unavoidable. Let's face the hard truth; at some point, every one of us is going to die, and at some point, each one of will have an experience of loss that thrust us into the grieving process.

Pain and Guilt

Shock and denial helps provide emotional protection from being overwhelmed from the experience of pain all at once. The truth is, no matter how many books you read to explain which stage of the grieving process you are in, the pain is real and nothing readable will take away the pain or hurt associated with the experience, just let it happen, feel it—it will change your life and perspective forever. *Pain and guilt* are usually a phase that people move to after they come to grips with the reality that, yes, it's true, "the person that I love, has really died." It's important to stay in the present, your pain is real; avoid self-medicating with drugs or alcohol, even when you feel guilty about what you said or didn't say, what you did or didn't do with the person that has died. The unknown is frightening during the pain and guilt phase; it is true, things will never be the same again, but being present in this phase can help you deal with the here, now and the way ahead.

Anger and Bargaining

Anger and bargaining is a phase that has been known to have the biggest impact on the personality. People react differently, but some tend to place blame for the death on someone other than the person that has died. The phase is deeply rooted with the belief that someone else is ultimately responsible for the death. The writer cautions the survivor that placing blame, even when it's unspoken, will alter the relationship and could cause permanent damage to the person you might believe is at fault or could have prevented the death. This phase may cause some to release emotions that might appear as explosive reactions to even minor interactions; it's a phase that can be fluid with enormous amounts of tension. Others might respond by bargaining with unrealistic expected outcome, like the willingness to take the person's place or questioning why the loved one had to die. The bargaining can also consist of just wanting to spend more time with the person; this is a phase where it is a good idea to spend time with loved ones that are left or ask for help so that your anger and bargaining won't leave you in relationship reins and make you become avoidable to those who are still living and wanting to love you.

Depression

Getting stuck in anger and bargaining can lead you into complications in the grieving experience and create a grief reaction of various forms. Depression is normal reaction to the grieving process. When the day-to-day new normal sets in, reflecting on the past and the loss could lead to long periods of sadness, loneliness that manifest itself in the form of depression. Don't be alarmed; it is normal, and in most cases, it is temporary. It's a period when all your friends have stopped calling to encourage you or checking on you, some people talk to you as if the death never happened and you should be over it by now. It's a time when people turn inward and stop showing outward emotion, as they are embarrassed or believed that others are sick of seeing and hearing about their grief experience. Be encouraged, you are not alone; there is no set time frame for how long this or any process should take. Once again, people grieve differently; don't be afraid to seek treatment. It is typically brief in most cases, but it can help you experience progress, and eventually your physical symptoms will lessen and your depression will become bearable, and eventually, you will get to a point of acceptance and hope.

Acceptance and Hope

There is a point where you will eventually start to move on with life and get to an acceptance of the experience and what life and the future has to offer. Hopefully, you get the sense that life is still happening around you, and you learn to deal with the experience of death and you carefully examine your future and your right now experience that you are still among the living and you must choose to live even though it is a different life.

There are therapeutic remedies for those who seek psychological treatment to overcome the painful and distorted reaction to death. It is sometimes confusing when you seek therapy that conflicts or contradicts your belief in God, but God knows this. Cognitive therapy, which has been referred to a problem-solving therapy, offers tools to help with distorted thoughts that has influence over our behavior. If you have negative thoughts about what the future holds without the person that has died, there may a tendency to behave in a way that supports the negative thought. So if I believe that in a few months I will lose everything including my home because I can no longer afford to maintain the lifestyle I am accustomed to after the death of my husband, who was the provider, then I could allow my faulty negative thoughts of hopelessness to influence and control my actions, which could lead me to create my own demise, i.e., I stop paying the mortgage, the car note, etc. . . . dealing with the situation with a positive lens could have resulted in a different outcome. This is where *hope* takes the wheel, because finding a job, or praying for help, or selling something else, could help with a different outcome. Even therapists know that just thinking differently won't solve the problems that you might be facing, ask God for what you really need and for the plan on how to get it, then put it into action. Counseling and therapy has its benefits and they can help you with distorted thoughts about the future and help you refocus your thoughts on positive hopeful outcomes and help review your thoughts and memories that complicate the bereavement experiences. However, you must choose for yourself to live among the living, even though it is a different life, your presence is required here on earth, and God requires you to set your mind on heaven. Find joy, even in your sadness. There is no right or wrong way to grieve privately, each of us will have a different experience, but there is a way for a Christian to grieve publicly, James instructs us to "count it all Joy, when we find ourselves in difficult times." I am human, so I know that is one of the most difficult passages to comprehend or master in the flesh, the human experience is full of emotions that contradict our response to our right now, but God knows all, and if we trust that he has a wonderful plan for our pain, we might be able to understand that we will be better Christians when we experience earthly disappointments, despair, and pain. God has giving us a manuscript on how to live (the Holy Bible), and in the life manuscript, it can guide us on where we will ultimately end up after death (heaven or hell), it also assures us that death is inevitable and unavoidable, but there is nothing in the manuscript that suggest how long we will live, only that we must die an earthly death, yet even with all of the evidence that life will end, we are still never prepared for the loss of a loved one, no matter what we know or how many times we've said it, we are never prepared so when that times come just feel it, let life have its imperfect way. Ask God for understanding and guidance and just as no man knows day or the hour of the coming of the Lord, no man knows the day or hour of his own death. God promises when we experience a death of a loved one, He will be with us in our despair and deepest sorrow. He tells us, *"So don't worry, because I am with you. Don't be afraid, because I am your God. I will make you strong and will help you; I will support you with the right hand that saves you"* (Isaiah 41:10). Sometimes people will not experience one of the stages while others will experience all of the stages more than once. If you have a sad day and the next day you are full of hope, it's all right; every day, ask God to lead the day, ask him to order your steps, and don't be discouraged. If you are not grieving like other people, it's an individual experience, it's personal, you are being groomed for greatness. Experts have identified other strategies for coping with bereavement, but most require you to conduct a self-inventory every day, by ensuring you focus on self-care, which includes caring for your mind, body, and soul. You choose for yourself how you administer the self-care, but you must do it so you won't get stuck in the complications associated with grief.

Mind

Keep your mind focused on heaven. Feel the experience of grief; whatever emotion comes up, express the emotion, don't hold on to the feelings, let it have its way, if you need to cry, then cry, if you feel sad, then feel the sadness, the same for fear, anger, shame, or any other emotion that shows up in the grief experience; there are healing possibilities in allowing yourself to feel the emotions that show up. Thinking positive about the person and the memories can help you have a moveable breakthrough in the grief posture, but it might take a while. It's all right to redirect your thoughts to positive moments you might have spent with the person, i.e., a good vacation, a treasured memory, your hope to see the again in heaven. There is a therapeutic exercise called relabeling. You can change the labels that you place on the experience; for example, "I was blessed to have ever met the person," rather than "I have lost them forever," or rather than "I will never see them again". When we get to heaven, we are going to rejoice. It's just a shift in how we think about the person and the experience. The Bible says, God's peace will be with you when you are in the storms of life; your thoughts are powerful. He commands us to *"fix your thoughts on what is true, and honorable, and right and pure and lovely and admirable. Think about things that re excellent and worthy of praise" (Philippians 4:8, NIV).* You will receive God's peace, keep a clear mind, and avoid self-medicating with drugs and alcohol or negative self-talk and negative people who you know will make you focus on negative things and people. Paul tells us we can make it; just press through the right now. He says, *"I don't mean to say that I have already achieved these things or that I have already reached perfection. But . . . I focus on this one thing; Forgetting the past and looking forward to what lies ahead, I press on to reach the end of the race and receive the heavenly prize for which God, through Crist Jesus, is calling us" (Phil. 3:12–14).* Start claiming your new normal and believe that things will get better.

Body

Your body is a temple that the Holy Spirit dwells in that you have received from God. While you are grieving, your body might feel as if it belongs to someone else; the level of pain your heart and mind experiences can also be felt in your body. In fact, if you are not careful, your body will betray you as soon as it gets word that you have had a devastating experience of loss, heartache, or pain. The experience could place you in a temporary state of unknown where nothing feels normal, but it is important to continue to participate in normal activities. Keep praying or start praying. Continue to make important decisions to ensure that your body does not get stuck in the temporary state of shock. Be ready for every encounter; Satan is a bully, especially when we are distressed or in despair. Stay on top of your hygiene, make sure you get up every day, get dressed, make an effort to show up in your own life, because whether we want to embrace the truth or not, life is short and it will continue with or without you being an active player.

Spirit

Feed your spirit or what is commonly known as the soul. The soul, which is regarded as immortal, is the immaterial part of the human experience; it's internal and cannot be measured for intactness. It will live on beyond the physical existence. Guard your soul by staying connected to God; he will guide you through the darkness of the bereavement experience. Just as I explained earlier that life and death are intertwined, they are not separate experiences, they are connected; they are one human experience. Pray for peace and have faith that you will experience peace, and I guarantee you, God's peace will have its perfect way for the future. There are nine fruits of the spirit, some you exercise and others you seek. Joy is the fruit of the spirit that is not dependent on circumstances, and biblically speaking, joy is differentiated from happiness because it is not a reactive emotion that is rooted in something happening; it is a state of mind, an orientation of the heart. Joy is the fruit of the spirit that everyone can access, if they truly want to find it, and yes, you can find joy in midst of your storm. It has always been there, the inner cheerfulness that is multiplied abundantly when you seek it; it is the stuffing in the inside that is wrap in hope. The hope we have in God who heals the brokenhearted and answers those who cry out to him. Read Jeremiah 31:13, John 15:11, Psalms 143 and 147 in the Holy Bible, which is filled with prayers and promises of deliverance that will help you with today and hope for tomorrow.

Forgiving God
Meet James

James is the firstborn and the only male of his three siblings. He grew up in Lake Charles, LA, just two hours outside of Houston, Texas. His Father was a Baptist minister, born and raised in Houston, Texas, and his mother was a professor at Houston's Graduate School of Theology. James remembers him and his family spending lots of time in the car taking the two-hour drive back and forth to Houston when he was young to visit his grandparents on his father's side. His grandfather was also a Baptist minister in Houston, Texas, and his grandmother was a homemaker who always had something special cooked for her only grandson. James's father ministered at a small, local church in Lake Charles, and everyone in town knew him and his family, so there was no way he could get into mischief because the minute he did anything wrong, it would get back to his mother and father faster than he could make it home. James says growing up in the house with three sisters made him aware of how "super sensitive" women really are; he also said it made him aware of how generously loving and nurturing women are, but his father made it clear that those were feminine qualities and men should not behave in similar ways. His father was strict and ruled with an iron fist; he had a really loud, deep voice and would call his name with authority. He knew his father loved him, but he rarely showed affection toward him; however, his sisters were treated like they were precious gemstones; it was a different kind of upbringing. He knew he was being trained and his sisters were being showed love. James remembers his mother's response to him being the complete opposite; she was training the girls and nurturing him with patient love. His mother was soft-spoken and everything she said reeked of the type of love God expects from us all. Although James proclaimed that she was the "perfect mother" to him, he knew in his heart she was not perfect in all of her ways. James remembers sharing with his mother his desire to travel the world and go places that he had been introduced to in books, places that his imagination had made larger than life. His mother would always tell him that he could be anything he set his mind to be and he could go anywhere he set his heart to go, and James never forgot those words growing up; he knew he wanted to leave the small town of Lake Charles, so when the opportunity came, he joined the air force to become an airline pilot.

James studied hard and became a pilot for the air force, and although he wasn't stationed everywhere in the world he wanted, he did have the opportunity to travel to different places and countries. James accepted an assignment at Luke Air Force base in Arizona where he was stationed for over five years. While James was stationed in Arizona, he was living the dream and found himself smiling for no good reason other than his dreams were being realized as a result of his hard work and faith in his mother's words. When it was time for James to transfer, he made an appointment to get a complete physical, which was a normal routine of out processing to the next duty station. While he went through the process of going from department to department, radiology, internal medicine, cardiology, podiatry, blood work, fitness test, and on and on.

While James walked from department to department, he received a text on his phone from a friend just saying how he was going to be missed in Arizona. He said he remembered thinking how nice it was for people to express how much of a friend he had been while stationed in Arizona. So rather than delay the opportunity to express his gratitude for the kindness, he stopped in the middle of the hospital hallway and begin to answer the text of the friend and just as he pushed send, his friend had responded quickly, so he stared at the response and texted back again, never looking up to see that he was blocking the walkway of others. He recalled a soft voice saying, "Excuse me, I can tell you are involved in an important discussion, but the rest of us can't get by." He said he didn't really look up, he just said, "Oh, I'm so sorry," and moved to the side, and as the click of the shoes, passed him, he could smell her soft perfume that took his breath away. It was a smell that he wanted to smell forever, by the time he looked up, he could only see the back of her; he knew she was a hospital employee and that was all he knew. James said he continued his walk to the next department, looking for podiatry, the foot doctor, but he kept taking in the sweet smell, that seemed to linger in the air. He was given a brief examination, and then on to X-ray for his final check on an old foot injury, and just as he was leaving X-ray, he smelled the perfume again. This time, he started looking for the owner of the smell, and just as he was about to give up, she came around the corner, looked him in the eye, and said, "Oh, hey, the guy with the important business in the hallway." He just looked her in the eye and said, "Hello, I want to apologize again. I'm sorry about that, but can you tell me what kind of perfume you are wearing?"

She just looked at him and smiled, then she said, "Oh, you like that, hum? Yea, it drives people crazy, sorry, not going to tell you, so you can have some other women smelling like me."

He said, he thought her perfume drove him crazy, but her smile was more powerful than the perfume. He professed to her that he didn't have anyone other than his mother that he would buy the perfume for; they held a lengthy conversation. He told her he was being transferred to the Philippines, and she told him that she had just got to Arizona. He asked her if she was a nurse. She smiled and said, "No, I am one of the medical doctors here, but I am in the air force too."

They exchanged numbers and began what James called a cross-worlds courtship. He was all the way on the other side of the world and all he could think about was her. His only wish was that he had met her earlier or that he could have extended his stay in Arizona. They sent pictures back and forth, talked on the phone, FaceTimed, texted, and even wrote old-fashioned letters from time to time. On the occasional rare opportunities they would see each other in person, they would go out of their way to make it as special and romantic as possible, each seeming to try and out due the other. James's tour in the Philippines was two years, and just when the two years was ending, Adrian was informed that she was being extended in Arizona. She told James of her fate and he didn't know where he was going next, but he knew it was not going to be Arizona. James said he just remembered being so unsettled with the long-distant courtship, he knew he wanted to be closer to Adrian so that they could get to know each other better. He had hoped that Adrian was feeling the same way; he said he called her late at night. She answered the phone almost in a panic, "Is everything all right?"

He said he just became silent, "Yes, everything is all right. I can't sleep, I'm sorry to call you this late at night, but I just wanted to know if you still want to be in this relationship?" She was quiet, and she asked him if he had met someone else. He said no, then he asked her, had she; she said no. He said she seemed to have gotten annoyed and asked him, "What is all this about?" He said, he told her, "Be honest, I was hoping you and I could find a way to live in the same city, but I know I cannot come back to Arizona and you are staying there. I just think they are going to send me somewhere on the East Coast and that would make us be a part for another two or three years."

He went on to say, "I guess I'm questioning whether we can withstand another three years of long-distant dating." He said she just got quiet, didn't say anything, even when he said hello a few times, she still remained quiet, and all of a sudden, she said, "I'm still here, so are we breaking up?" He said he felt like a train had hit him when she asked that question, and the only response he could give her is "I guess so." He said before he could even process the information she had hung up the phone. He tried calling her over and over again; he felt stupid. "Why didn't I just tell her that she was the love of my life, and no, we are not breaking up? I am going to find a way to fix it."

The words just came out; before he knew it, he didn't mean it, but no matter how many times he tried calling her, she would not answer the phone. He sent her instant messages, text, Facebook post, still no response. James realized that he couldn't concentrate at work, couldn't sleep, or eat; he was heartbroken all because he didn't tell her what he was really trying to say. One of his good friends said, "Man, get control of yourself, you are moping around, acting like you lost your best friend. You are a hopeless case and the best thing that he could do was to take some time off and get on a plane and tell her how you really feel, you have nothing to lose at this point." James tried calling her again, but got no answer, so James took his friends advice and got a HOP back to the States.

It had been three weeks since that middle of the night phone call that had him in agony and despair. He set out to make it right; he got in early so he went straight to her house, which she shared with a roommate. Her roommate informed him that she was working a double shift and was still at the hospital. Her roommate also said, "You might want to call first. I don't know how happy she is going to be to see you." Her comment cut deep, but he also knew she was not taking his calls, so he drove over to the hospital. When he stepped off the elevator and turned the corner, he could smell her; he knew she was near. He just kept checking every room, and the scent got stronger and stronger, and finally, he was standing right behind her. He said that if she was mad at him; she still lit up when she turned around, and he just knew, whatever she was feeling before, his face-to-face presence broke through all her resentment. He said she smiled, then he smiled; the next thing he knew, he was on one knee, asking her to spend the rest of her life with him, and all the other mushy stuff that happens when you know that this person is the one!

Adrian and James were married in Lake Charles, Louisiana, at the church that his parents and his grandparents were married in. It was small, but perfect. They were able to get military orders to station them in the same city in San Antonio, Texas. James said he had never experienced such a forgiving spirit as Adrian; she always made everything seem easy. Her favorite line was, "Don't worry about it, you'll get through it." She had a strong faith in God; she always reminded him who the real pilot was in their relationship. When things got heated in their discussion, she would say, "Jesus, take the wheel," and it always made heavy conversations light. They bought a small but nice starter house in a suburb, Shavano Park, near San Antonio, Texas. James was sent on an assignment and Adrian was working at the nearby hospital; this time, it was labor and delivery, where she had the opportunity to spend time with babies and new mothers. This assignment kept him away from time to time, but never more than a month at a time; when he was home, they were together all the time. James remembers thinking time was flying; it had already been three years since they had got married. He said he believed all they ate and drank was *love* for the first two years of the marriage, and it felt like that was all they needed.

James remembers coming home late from an assignment, and when he walked in the house, it was completely dark. He kept calling Adrian's name because he had talked to her when his plane landed, and she said she was on her way home. He called out to her one more time, and finally she answered; she told him she was in the bathroom. He said she came running out of the bathroom with some object in her hand, screaming, "We did it, we did it."

He asked, "We did what?"

She said, in the most caring, soft voice, "We are pregnant. We are going to have a baby!" James said he was speechless; they had talked about it casually a few times, but he figured she only mentioned it because she was working in labor and delivery and was starting to deliver lots of babies for other families, but she didn't seem to make a big deal about it, nor did she seemed obsessed, so it was a shock to see the amount of joy that this had brought her. James remembers being excited and shocked at the same time. After a day or so, he felt just as excited as she Adrian. They called their families, her mother first, who had been asking that question since the wedding, "When am I going to be a grandmother?" So when she heard the news, she screamed so loud they were both stunned by the excitement. Then they called his parents who were just as loud as Adrian's mother; all of them were excited. James put all three of his sisters on the phone together because he knew that he couldn't tell one first because they would start bragging about who knew first; they all screamed at the same time and were equally happy.

James said time was going fast, and Adrian was preparing for motherhood; she was taking it serious, reading books about childrearing, eating healthy, and breastfeeding. She had convinced James to start getting the baby's room ready. She seemed to be having a fairly normal pregnancy, although her cravings were far from normal. She would ask James to get combinations of things that just didn't seem to go together, like ice cream and a can of Pink Salmon, or strawberries and wheat bread, and when he would ask her, "Do you want them both together?" She would become very sensitive, and from time to time, she would just start crying for what he believed was no good reason at all; everything else seemed to be normal. James said Adrian loved to have him feel the movement of the baby, who, after about six months, became very active. Adrian and James agreed they did not want to know the sex of the baby; they wanted to just wait and be surprised at the delivery, but it did make setting the room up restrictive. Adrian said, "Just paint the room off white, and from there, that color set the tone for everything else, including the baby's bed, and all the other things needed for the room."

Adrian's mother had planned to come and stay with them for the first two months after the baby was delivered so she could help Adrian and James. When James's mother heard that Adrian's mother was coming, she made a request to come and help out too, although she had only planned to stay one month; she didn't want Adrian's mother to have the jump start on grand-babying, so it was agreed they were both coming. Adrian and James's mothers had become good friends over the years, so they were both looking forward to the fellowship, friendship, and the baby's arrival to enhance the visit. Adrian's mother had repeatedly said the first baby was always late, and in order to maximize her time and prove her point, she made her travel arrangements to arrive the day after the designated due date of the baby. While James's mother got there two days before Adrian's scheduled due date, her thinking was sometimes the first baby's come early. It was New Year's Eve, they had planned to spend a quiet evening at home, but all their friends insisted that they come over and have game night to bring in the New Year. James prepared a few appetizers and picked up out-of-place items in the room. They were excited to have his mom there; the minute she stepped foot in the house, she started helping out around the house. She cleaned up and prepared the appetizers and made sure that Adrian was comfortable. She didn't let her lift a thing. "I'll do it, don't put any strain on yourself, you got my grandbaby to worry about."

The evening was fun; they had about eight friends over. They played games, discussed work events, possible baby names, politics, and everything that you can think of. Adrian was feeling tired and said she could not make it until the twelve o'clock hour for the coming of the New Year; it was about 10:45 PM and she told James to come and get her at 11:50 PM. She said, "Please don't let me miss the countdown. All I need is a little nap." James promised, and the small gathering continued with more laughs and stories. James's mother reminded James to wake Adrian up. She told James, "It's eleven fifty, and you promised, so keep your promise." James's first reaction was, "She really needs the rest. She only has two more days to go, and she will never get to rest again for years." He told his mother, "I think I will just let her sleep."

His mother said it again, "Keep your promise." When James looked at his mother, he knew that there was something serious about her words, so he got up and went into the room where Adrian was sleeping and gently woke her up, saying, "Adrian, it's almost midnight, wake up, baby." Adrian jumped up, excited, and the first thing she said was, "Aww, you kept your promise, thanks for not letting me miss the start of the New Year. It's my favorite thing to do." She got up so fast James had to tell her, "You can slow down, you still have about seven minutes." She came back out and joined the party and everyone was happy to see her. Adrian was excited; they had opened champagne and cider and poured it into the glasses and all James could do was thank his mother for insisting that he wake Adrian up. She started, she informed the room, two minutes, one minute, then finally . . . 10, 9, 8, 7, 6, 5, 4, 3, 2, 1—"HAPPY NEW YEAR!" They hugged, kissed, and each of them clinked their glasses together. Someone started chanting, words, words, words, so James's good friend David started by raising his glass and shouting, "May the 365 days be better than the last 365 days." Everyone in the room repeated his words and took a drink (an old tradition of the military), another one of the guest shouted, "To being the next pregnant person in the room" everyone started to repeat what she said and thought about it, then her husband confirmed, Adrian shouted, "Oh my goodness, our children will grow up together and play together." They had been saving the news for the new year . . . . They lifted their glasses again and shouted, "To pregnancy," with a roar of laughter at once; they repeated the toast, "To pregnancy." James's mother held her glass up next, "To a year of new beginnings," and the repeating continued. When it was Adrian's turn, she said, "To another year with good friends and family." Then it was James's turn and everyone thought he was going to say something funny, but with all seriousness, he looked Adrian in the eyes, raised his glass high, and said, "TO LOVE"; everyone repeated, "TO LOVE." Adrian was all choked up and tears started to fall; she kept her eyes locked on James and said, with her glass raised high, "TO LOVE!"

Everyone kept talking for a little while longer, passed the midnight countdown, and around 1:00 AM, they all started to gather their things and saying their goodbyes; each one asked to be informed the minute that Adrian went into labor, some left with comments about naming the baby after them; if it's a boy or girl on their way out the door, another said, "Don't let me read that the baby is born on Facebook. I want a call." Adrian agreed that a personal call would be made to each one of the house guest, or one of them would call or text all of them. Once all the guests had left, her mother-in-law instructed her to go back to bed and don't worry about cleaning up. She told her that she and James would take care of the house, so Adrian went back to sleep and James and his mother started cleaning up the kitchen. James put away all the games, and he and him mother talked about family and friends and how life was about to change when the baby came. When they finished cleaning up, he and his mother hugged and James thanked her and told her how happy he was that she was there. When James got to bed, Adrian was sound asleep, and all he could do is smile. He was happy that he kept his promise and he could tell she was fulfilled by being able to participate in the countdown and the festivities. James said he had not realized that this was only the second New Year's Eve they had ever spent together and the first one as husband and wife; he never thought too much of the day and did not realize how much it meant to Adrian, but he was glad his mother said, "Keep your promise." Mother is always right."

The next day was New Year's Day, it was just the three of them, and it was a quiet and intimate day of more talking and reminiscing about childhood events, mostly James's mischief and some of the ways he treated his sisters' boyfriends when they would come over. James's mother talked about how fast children grow up and what to expect through the years. They laughed until they cried. James's mother was so excited; this was her first grandchild from her beloved son. Around noon, Adrian's mother called, reporting that she would be arriving on January 4, even though the due date was January 2; she teased that she wished she would have just come early and she could have spent New Year's Eve and New Year's Day with them. "What was I thinking?" she asked. "Don't have too much fun without me." Adrian put her on speaker phone so she was able to talk them all at the same time, then Adrian took the phone and had a private conversation with her mother. She told her mother she was scared and she couldn't wait until she came. Adrian kept rubbing her back; by 9:00 PM, she started to complain that she was having some serious discomfort in her back. James's mother said, "That's how it starts for some people. You can go for a walk, and it will help with the labor pains and movement of the baby." Adrian thought it was a good idea; they set out to take a walk around the block. The more they walked, the more she complained about her discomfort. She said, "I am really in pain. Do you think this is it?"

Her mother-in-law said, "It could be, it is the date they said." Around 11:00 PM, Adrian was feeling better and the pain had calmed down, so she laid down and went to sleep. Around 4:30 AM, she woke James up. She said, "I think we should call the doctor and go to the hospital. I can't take the pain anymore." James hadn't realized she was even in any pain, so he just looked at her at first, not realizing what was going on. Suddenly, he jumped up and he and Adrian realized that her water had broken and it really was time. January 2,

Adrian's exact due date, and she begin to experience labor pains in an indescribable way. She had delivered many babies in the labor and delivery room; she knew what to tell women, what to expect, but when you are the one in pain, it is a completely different experience. James's mother kept them both calm; she was experienced, and this was a very familiar reaction to a firstborn child. James was nervous and running around the house like he was on fire. Adrian and her mother-in-law kept looking at each other, but they never exchanged words. Finally, Adrian asked her mother-in-law to call her mother, to tell her we are on our way to the hospital. Her mother-in-law made the call. Adrian's mother just shouted "no"; the first baby never comes on time. "I am so mad at myself. Okay. let's see if I can change my flight, keep me posted. I'm going to call the airlines right now." Adrian's mother-in-law started making phone calls to the people they had promised, including her three daughters. "We are on our way to the hospital. The baby wants out." She laughed. Adrian's old roommate said she was going to meet them at the hospital. James asked his mother to call the hospital. "All you need to say is Adrian's water broke and we are on our way." Adrian had worked in the labor and delivery department for a few years and was well known by everyone; they were all her people. They knew what to do.

James was frantic and would not calm down, while Adrian was in pain and just shook her head. James really was glad that her mother-in-law was there to tend to things that they were overlooking, like closing the garage door, getting her bags, and calling the hospital. When James's mother finally called the hospital, she had to tell the person on the other end Adrian's last name and more information than they all expected. Adrian said, "Oh yea, it's Saturday and the day after New Year's. No one is going to be at work. They took the day off." Those who were at work got the news fast, and they were all excited and ready for her.

When Adrian got to the hospital, her doctor was waiting for her; he took her right into the room to examine her. He told her it would be a while; she had only dilated to five centimeters. The doctor also told her, "You know the routine. We will keep you comfortable, and I will come back in to check on you. A few minutes later, James's mother's phone rang. It was Adrian's mother stating that she had gotten a flight out and would be there in about four hours. James's mother told her, "I think you got plenty of time. She is only five centimeters." She said she would catch a cab and come straight to the hospital and would call again when she landed. James said it felt like time had stood still; he kept walking back and forth in the room where Adrian was waiting patiently for the baby to cooperate. Her old roommate, Cassandra, had made to the hospital and began to call all their close friends, and some asked her to keep them posted, while others started arriving at the hospital, even those who actually worked there and had the day off, no one wanted to be left off. The waiting room started to look like a small party after about three hours. Some people came and others left; James kept asking Adrian if there was anything he could do. She kept saying, "I'm fine" until a contraction hit, and a loud moan would follow. It was overwhelming for James to see her in so much pain. James told him, "Mother, this is way too long. It's been over six hours that she has been in labor. James's mother said, "Well, I was in labor with you for over twelve hours." James had heard his mother say that many times, but this was the first time he ever realized the magnitude of the time; he just could not understand how women could take that many hours of pain. As he and his mother were talking, Adrian's mother walked into the room. She had arrived with all the luggage in tow; after all, she was staying for two months. When Adrian saw her mother, she started to cry and kept saying, "You made it, Mom, you made it. I needed you here. Thanks so much for coming, you made it!" Her mother started to cry too and said, "You know I wouldn't miss my only girl's first childbirth experience, you knew I was coming."

They hugged and her mother kept kissing her, then her mother told James to take a break and go into the lobby because it looked like a party out there. "Give the people an update. They seem restless," she proclaimed. Adrian was on her ninth hour of labor when the doctor reported that she had reached the magic number of ten centimeters, and he wanted to prep her for delivery. Both mothers left out of the room, and James was dressed and draped for the big event. James's mother went into the lobby and made the big announcement, "It's time, it's just a matter of minutes." Everyone was so excited. James's mother was right. It was a matter of minutes. It's a girl, "Sarah Rene," and she was beautiful, nine pounds, three ounces, the biggest baby in the family. They cleaned her up and everyone was so excited; by this time, it was 2:20 PM on January 2, and James and Adrian had their firstborn little baby girl. James announced that this had to be the happiest day of his life. The nurse staff said they were going to move the baby to the nursery so all the family and friends could get a chance to see her. Everyone headed to the nursery. James was behind the glass (one of the benefits of your wife working in the labor and delivery). Everyone made baby noises at her. James's mother said, "She is finally here and what a beautiful baby."

After they played with the baby for a while, James and his mother alone with a few others said they were going to the cafeteria for some much-needed food. Adrian's mother said she had already eaten on the plane and was going back in the room to see how Adrian was doing, she noticed how exalted she was, and she knew she needed some sleep. As she was headed to the room, she noticed the emptiness of the hallway; she reflected on her own experience of childbirth. She remembered the day she gave birth to Adrian. As she was walking, she felt on overwhelming sense of pain go through her body. She couldn't take in air, much like a panic attack or hyperventilating. As she was walking down the hallway, she felt as if she was going to collapse, and she knew she needed to sit down. The hospital was short of staff, and no one was around. Eventually, she just grabbed the back of a chair and held on to it; she felt as if all her breath had been taken out of her body. She felt like time was standing still and she could see herself outside of herself. She managed to turn the chair around and sit down; eventually, a doctor was just passing by and asked her if she was all right. She explained to him that she felt like she was on the verge of collapsing, and she felt light-headed. He called for some additional help, and they put her on a gurney and began to ask her a series of questions, mostly to find out if she was coherent and aware of where and who she was. She told him that her daughter and son-in-law had just had a baby, and she was fine; she may have been excited or jet-lagged.

She could hear voices and commotion going on down the hall, then she heard a scream. The doctor told her, "Stay here, don't move." She wasn't sure where the screams were coming from, but she knew it wasn't a good scream. Just as was trying to lift up, James, his mother, and some of the others came walking down the hallway. James could see she was on a gurney and started to run toward her just as he was running toward his mother-in-law. Adrian's doctor started walking toward them all. He watched her doctor and tried to tend to his mother-in-law at the same time. James asked her what was wrong and what was going on. She started to tell him that she felt as if she was going to collapse, and the next thing she knew, she got light-headed and a doctor and a few others came and put her on the gurney. Adrian's doctor gave James a melancholy look, and then he asked if he could talk to him. He started by saying, "All of a sudden, there were some complications. We tried everything to revive her."

James just stared at him and said, "She was so healthy. I was just holding her—NO, this can't be happening." James could hear the commotion coming from Adrian's room. "Did you tell her?" His mother started to cry. Adrian's mother started to cry, and just as James started running toward Adrian's room, the doctor ran after him, and said, "James, the baby is fine, the baby is fine. It's Adrian who experienced the complications. We just couldn't stop the bleeding. We did everything we could. We couldn't save her. James, we lost her, I'm so sorry, I'm so sorry."

James looked back at his mother and his mother-in-law, and he knew they didn't have a clue what the doctor had just said. He knew they believed it was Sarah Rene who was no longer with them. He couldn't move; he was standing three feet away from Adrian's room. He could hear the commotion coming out of the room, but he couldn't move. The baby was down the other hall, and all he could think of is what just happened. In a matter of one hour, the best day of his life just turned into the worst day of his life. How could these two feeling collide on the same day at the same time? He just kept looking at his mother and his mother-in-law. He heard the doctor, "The baby is doing fine." Adrian's mother starting getting off the gurney with James's mother's help, and James was frozen in his tracks. Adrian's doctor kept whispering his name, "James, James." No response. "James, they are cleaning her up now, so you guys can go in and see her and say your goodbyes."

James never moved or blinked; he said it again, "James." No response. "James, should I tell her mother and the others that the baby is fine, or do you want to tell them?" Just as the doctor asked that question, Adrian's old roommate came over and put are arms around James. She whispered in his ear, "It's okay. You guys can try again. I know it hurts, but God will give you guys another baby." Her words cut him deep. He looked at her and said, "No we can't. She died, Karen! We will never have another baby. It was Adrian that died, Karen, it was Adrian." Karen just dropped her arm from James and shouted, "WHAT?" Everyone in earshot let out a loud gasp. Adrian's mother screamed, "Oh my God! No! Not my baby, no." James's mother ran toward him; she grabbed him and just hugged him. He couldn't move, he couldn't cry, he could think, he couldn't even hear, he saw the commotion. He knew he was witnessing a tragedy, but he could not imagine being a part of the tragedy. This was not happening to him. James couldn't imagine her being gone; he couldn't imagine living without her, he could feel the lost deep inside of him, and he felt empty. James was still standing in the same place outside of the room; he still had not moved, he could hear Adrian's mother wailing. She was saying she would take her place and she kept asking, "How could this happen?" James's mother tried consoling him. She kept trying to talk to him; he wouldn't respond. He just stood there. All of a sudden, something shook him; he seemed to come back to the tragedy and he remembered his daughter. He called for one of Adrian's co-workers who seemed to be in as much grief as he was. He asked her, "Can you go, and if she could go and get our baby, can you go and get her please? I don't want to go in there without her." The doctor said it was fine. The whole experience was happening in the hallway of the labor and delivery room of the hospital. James still had never moved. He waited. Once he had the baby in his hands, he felt like she already knew that her mommy was no longer with them. He felt this overwhelming desire to console her, to assure her that she had nothing to do with her mother's death. He just kept looking at her and he felt like she was talking to him. He remembered thinking, "What are we going to do, Sarah? What are we going to do? I should have been paying attention to all the things she was saying. What are we going to do?" Then there was another overwhelming desire to protect her; he walked in Adrian's room with Sarah in his hand, and he saw Adrian lying there as if she was sleep. He knew if Adrian could say anything to him at the moment, she would say, "You're going to be all right. You can do it, you are doing to figure this out. It will all be fine, have faith." She always had encouraging words. James didn't really know if he believed he would be all right, or if he could do it, but at that moment, he needed to just breathe and make it past the moment in front of him. James told me that "Everyone wanted to take the baby and hold her while I say my goodbyes, but I never let her go. I just held on to the baby. I just kept holding on. I kept hearing the same question over and over again, 'Do you want me to take her?' I kept saying, no, I got her. What they didn't know was, I wasn't holding the baby, the baby was holding me. I knew if I would have let her go, I would have fell. I just looked at Adrian for a long time, not sure why this was happening to me, why was I experiencing this level of pain. Why did God take my loving wife, what was I going to do without her? What was I going to do with this little baby girl? I just held her tight, I held her for seven days nonstop. I even held her when I ate, and when she was asleep. The only time I put her down was to get dressed and to use the bathroom. Holding her was the only way I could avoid thinking about my new reality and avoid answering questions about what I was going to do. My grief and the grief that is to come for my baby girl absorbed my thoughts. I kept asking God why, and when I didn't get an answer, I started to avoided God, and I could feel bitterness creeping in, when anyone would say something like, lean on God, and God loves you. He will be there for you. I knew God loved me, but I still asked the question, why did God allow me to experience such devastation and joy at the same time. If all things work for the good of those who love God, then what good could possible come out of this situation and this level of pain?"

UNEXPECTED TURBULENCE

The days following the death of Adrian, James had many things to do concerning his life—fatherhood, his grief, and the future. At the funeral, many people expressed their heartfelt condolences; there were so many sad faces. Grief had taken his toll on everyone in their lives, including both of their families. James had never felt this level of grief, and he knew he could not concentrate, so he took life in increments of seconds. He made through those thirty seconds; soon it was a minute, and then on to the hour. James could remember praying for a baby; more importantly, even though he had not told Adrian, he wanted it to be a baby girl. God had answered his prayer, but he was not sure why his answered prayer had cost him so much. He was angry, hurt, and grateful all at the same time. He didn't know what to do next, and he needed time figure it out, so he took an indefinite leave of absences from work. His superiors supported his request and told him to take his time so that he could figure it all out.

For months, James and his baby were not home alone; his mother, his mother-in-law, and one of his sisters stayed with him and Sarah Rene; it was as if they had created a life schedule that allowed everything to run smoothly, including the feedings, changings, and meals. They were all naturals, and at times, they would tag team on chores without saying a word to each other. James's mother-in-law was grieving; she had lost her baby girl and was staring at the reincarnation of her baby girl through the eyes of Sarah Rene. She missed her daughter, and when the time was right, she asked James if she could take Sarah Rene home with her. She offered to keep her while he attempted to get himself ready to return to work, which might require him to be away from home from time to time. She promised him she would take good care of her, and that he could come and visit at any time he wanted. James had not prepared himself for a conversation like this, and he didn't want to hurt his mother-in-law's feelings, but he was not in agreement with his daughter being in a different state than him. He just looked at her and gave her a long-lasting hug, then he told her, "She is not Adrian; Adrian is gone. I promise you, I am going to figure this whole thing out. I know you mean well, but I cannot image living without my daughter after losing my wife." His mother-in-law said she understood and admitted she was heartbroken and thought that Sarah Rene could help fill the empty void she was experiencing. His mother-in-law had already packed her bags and said she needed to go home. A few days later, James's own mother made the same declaration; it was time for her to go home too. James's youngest sister decided to stay another week to help him stay organized and to find childcare that he was comfortable with. The baby seemed to be growing overnight. At times, James would stare at Sarah Rene for long periods of time without saying a word. He questioned how he was going to raise her without her mother; what was he going to tell her? What was he going to do?

James said he never really got any sleep, he found himself replaying his life over and over again; he kept questioning what went wrong, what could he have done to have a different outcome. Him and his sister never had to cook, friends and co-workers of Adrian and his own co-workers were amazing in every way. They brought baby clothes, food, diapers; he had not been alone with the baby in weeks. James never contemplated anything like this happening; he and his thoughts were strangers, and he was a stranger in his new life. He had a new baby and no wife. James said he remembers avoiding God, everyone kept saying they were praying for him and Sarah Rene, and he kept thinking, "Well, lots of people are praying for us, so the praying is being taken care of. He couldn't or wouldn't stop to thinking about why God let his wife die. He kept hearing himself ask why. How could this happen, how could God let this happen? Everyone played a major role in getting through the day, but James admits he kept asking, where was God? How could he allow such devastation and pain? What did I do wrong? Why me? Why us? Why, God? Why? James's heart was broken and his faith was shaken. He was filled with questions that made him ashamed of his thoughts about God's purpose and God's will. It's natural for humans to question God's way and his will in the midst of despair. We want what we want, and we want God to want us to have what we want, and during those times of unexpected turbulence, we question why he has disrupted our plans for our lives. We question whether we are experiencing God the judge. Did we do something that we are now experience repayment on? Is God judging our lives, our sins, and thus punishing us for what we have done? Are we reaping the bad seed we have sown? I don't make many promises, but I promise that is not why the living experience death. It is inevitable and a part of life. You and everyone you know will die; the only thing that is questionable is when and I assure you, if you are living, no matter how or who, you will not be ready for it.

Think back to a time when you thought this was the worst experience that could ever happen, and you didn't know how you were going to live through it, but you made it and you are still here. Never give up even when you have a bad day, a bad week, or even a bad month, never give up! James asked himself where God was when his storm rolled in—where was God? David gave us some encouragement on how to present ourselves when the storms are raging, he says in Psalms 23:4, *"Even though I walk through the valley of the shadow of death, I will fear no evil, for you are with me; your rod and your staff, they comfort me."* God was with James and baby Sarah Rene during their experience of the loss of Adrian. He was there then and is still with them now; all they have to do is just trust and believe God's promises.

Grief has shaken James's faith; he said, at times he can be cynical. He finds himself making comments like "There ain't no happy endings," and as soon as he says it, he remembers the gift that God has given him, sweet little "Sarah Rene," who looks so much like her mother; that it takes his breath away when she smiles. James says sometimes he looks at her and he asks God, "What are you thinking? What is your plan for us? What am I going to do, Lord?" He said on other days, he tells the Lord what he has promised. "Lord, you said you would never forsake them. Help me to not feel forsaken today." James said he knew he couldn't just sit down and mourn because it would put him a paralyzed state, and he would never get back up again; he also knew that God knew that losing his wife, his soul mate, his friend was such a gut-wrenching, emotional trauma that he gave him a grief to be responsible for, and he has made it his promise to Adrian and God that he is going to take care of this small little baby girl, who depends on him for everything. It is God's way of keeping him in the here and now; there is no time for never-ending mourning. Even with his deep sorrow, he had to be present for his daughter. He is a father, her life is in his hands for now. "HELP ME, LORD, TO MAKE IT THROUGH. I have received the best gift in my life that is known to man by way of the worst tragedy that is uncomprehendable. How could the best day and the worst day of my life collide?"

"IF ONLY"
MEET BARBARA

Barbara is a second oldest in a family of seven, the oldest girl of the seven. Barbara grew up in a small city outside the St. Louis area. Her mother was married to Barbara's father, but when Barbara was young, her mother and father divorced. Barbara remembers her father as an active participant in her life by way of weekend visits that were used to show her and her siblings that he really was a good father. Barbara said she never remembers her mother saying anything negative about her father, not even when her mother and father first divorced. Barbara is considered the matriarch of her sibling family, and most of her family gatherings are centered around Barbara and her home.

Barbara is a sixty-seven-year-old African American woman who is known for being outspoken and for speaking her truth, no matter what others think. She as a gift for giving most people know she has a big heart, and she usually is giving most people she comes in contact with something to eat because she loves to cook for anyone who is hungry. Barbara is the mother of three adult males, and while she was in St. Louis, she married and separated from her oldest son's Dewayne, father. After her separation with Dewayne's father, she had two more sons Reggie and her youngest son Kendrick. Barbara moved to Chicago and was the sole provider for three of her young sons. They lived in Chicago for about eight years and eventually moved to California where she currently resides. Barbara admits that raising three sons alone in California in a high-risk neighborhood known for requiring young boys to prove themselves on a daily basis was a challenge. Barbara worked hard to teach her young boys right from wrong, good from bad. Once Barbara was settled into the neighborhood, her second eldest son met and mated with one of the girls in the neighborhood who lived directly across the street from their house. That relationship made Barbara a grandmother at the age of thirty-seven and her middle son Reggie a father at the age of nineteen. Reggie's son was his namesake and was affectionate, known as Lil Reggie. The close proximity of the two families made it possible for both families to share in the upbringing of Lil Reggie, and Barbara made it clear that she was going to be an active participant. When Lil Reggie was about five months old, his mother took him to spend the night with one of her family members for a few days. Barbara started looking for her and Lil Reggie, and when she found them she noticed that Lil Reggie looked like he needed medical attention, so she took Lil Reggie with her, and after getting him home, she took Lil Reggie to a local hospital who refused him treatment but offered to call an ambulance to transport him to another hospital. Barbara said her and her youngest son Kendrick decided to drive Lil Reggie to the hospital themselves, and when they got there, it was clear that Lil Reggie was gravely ill and was in need of immediate medical attention. Lil Reggie was admitted into the hospital, treated and diagnosed with spinal meningitis and dehydration, among other things. Spinal meningitis in infants is an infection of the fluid of a person's spinal cord and the fluid that surrounds the brain. It is usually caused by a viral or bacterial infection. The severity of the illness differs in each individual depending on whether it is caused by a virus or bacterium. Although Lil Reggie's case was less severe than some, he stayed in the hospital for over a week and the doctors informed the family that had he not come to the hospital when he did it was not likely that he would have survived. When Lil Reggie was released, he was released to Barbara, his grandmother, not his biological mother. Barbara brought Lil Reggie's home with her and became his unofficial caregiver and guardian. Barbara shares that Lil Reggie's biological mother made attempts to take and keep Lil Reggie across the streets to her house, but every time she tried, she would have to bring him back because Lil Reggie would cry the entire time he was in her care, and she could not stop him or handle it. Barbara and Lil Reggie's mother had no formal agreement or never discussed guardianship over Lil Reggie; it was just known that Lil Reggie lived with his Grandmother Barbara, whom he affectionately referred to as "Granny"! Barbara and her sons made a commitment to keep the baby and raise him without any assistance from anyone, including is biological mother and with the help of her sons and other family members, including her goddaughter and neighbor downstairs. Barbara became the caregiver for Lil Reggie, and he never returned to the care of his biological mother.

Lil Reggie grew up in the same neighborhood as his mother, but he rarely had contact with his mother or any of his family members on his mother side of the family. Many days, his mother would pass right by him while he was outside playing, and although she offered a friendly wave, it was not evident that he was exchanging pleasantries with his biological mother. In fact, many times she didn't even seem to notice Lil Reggie playing outside; he would say after she had passed by, "There go my mama." When Lil Reggie was about seven years old, his mother had given birth to Lil Reggie's sister and Lil Reggie would ask his granny if he could go across the streets to play with his sister, and sometimes he would even ask to spend the night with his mother and sister, but Lil Reggie would never last throughout the night; he would start his ritual, "I want to go with my Granny, take me home, call my granny," and he would not stop until someone either took him home, or someone across the street came and got him. Barbara says this went on for years; it was a known fact that Lil Reggie would not sleep over at anyone's house, except maybe his close friends' house downstairs from Granny, where he could walk upstairs at any time if he wanted to come home. Lil Reggie had his ways growing up; he was close to the granny and his granny's side of the family. Barbara shared a story about Lil Reggie having a ring when he was around six or seven years old, and when people would ask to see his ring, he would hold the ring up to their face, and say, "See it with your eyes," because he was not going to take the ring off as he was instructed by his granny. Lil Reggie also grew up trying to rap on the mic every chance he got; he had professed that he was going to be a rapper when he grew up, and he would entertain the family as often as he could with his new rhymes, even if it was just two lines. Lil Reggie had a reputation for watching everything that was going on around him; he paid attention and would either repeat it back to you or demonstrate it through his actions. He learned how to cook when he was very young, and he was given daily chores around the house growing up and was no stranger to hard work because of his granny.

By the time Lil Reggie got in high school, like other boys his age, he started to experiment with trouble and hanging with the wrong crowd; his uncle and aunt offered him an opportunity to attend his last year in high school in a slower-pace city; it was there that Lil Reggie got in trouble with the authorities, and he ended up back home to his granny. Lil Reggie's struggled with his grades in high school, and after his run-in with the authorities, he ended up in a continuation school, with all odds against him. Lil Reggie was determined to get his high school diploma, and even though it took him to work hard in his senior year, he finished the work needed and got his high school diploma. Lil Reggie was a prankster and loved to laugh; he was a nice guy who from time to time made some bad choices. When Lil Reggie was about twenty-four years old, he got into a serious relationship with a young lady; basically, it was love his way. Lil Reggie could not be found without her and the same with her unless they were at work. Barbara and her sons opened up a family restaurant where all her sons and Lil Reggie worked together. It was hard work, but none of them are stranger to hard work. What the family noticed is Lil Reggie picked up a drinking habit that seemed innocent enough at first, but as time went on, he started showing up at family events beyond the acceptable social drinking levels, and it became concerning to Barbara, so she would tell him to know and control his limit, but his drinking became progressively worst. Lil Reggie's girlfriend started complaining about his drinking, and he was aware that everyone wanted him to cut back on his drinking in public and at the family social events because everybody knew how and who he was without alcohol. After some years had passed, the family business closed and Lil Reggie and his girlfriend broke up, which may have caused Lil Reggie to drink more. Lil Reggie started making promises that he was going to stop drinking, and it was clear that he wanted to stop, but it just seemed as if he didn't know how. Lil Reggie once again was living with his granny, and in August, he came to a birthday party for his auntie and said he was given his auntie a gift that he was going to stay sober for her party and he did just that. In September, Lil Reggie started acting out and appeared to be upset a lot; his cousin described his behavior as "just strange"—no other way to explain it. His Granny had gotten a call from a family friend that Lil Reggie was drunk in public, just talking loud and stumbling, so she asked the friend to put Lil Reggie on the phone, so she could talk to him. She asked him what was wrong with him and why he was drunk in the streets. She told him to come home and to stop acting up. The family friend gave him a ride home, brought him home, and when he got there, he went straight to sleep. The next morning, he didn't remember much of anything from the day before, but it was clear he was binge drinking and was unhappy about something. Barbara was concerned about Lil Reggie, but she believed that "this too shall pass"; after all, he had promised he was going to stop drinking and had started to ask questions about alcoholism and recovery. Barbara was preparing for a trip to Jamaica she had planned for over a year. She kept talking to Lil Reggie as she packed about his behavior, his choices, his life, like all young adults, he knew the answers, and of course, he was going to handle his business and himself. Mostly because of Lil Reggie's binge drinking, Barbara decided she was not going to leave Lil Reggie at her house while she was gone; she told him she wanted him to stay over her sister's house while she was gone to Jamaica on vacation. Lil Reggie and his granny had words; he said he was going to stay at his girlfriend's house, and he explained that he was a grown man and he would do what he wanted to do.

Barbara left on a Friday going to Jamaica and Lil Reggie had a change of heart and went to Barbara's sister's house, where the rest of the family was meeting for a birthday party and to watch the fight. Lil Reggie approached one of his cousins and told her that he needed help with his drinking and that this was going to be his last time drinking. Lil Reggie and his cousin found an in-patient treatment center and they agreed to take Lil Reggie on the following Monday. Lil Reggie made his big announcement to the whole family and told them that he was going to make his Granny proud when she came back from her vacation, he knew all she wanted for him was for him to be safe. That night, which was declared as Lil Reggie's last time drinking, he started celebrating by drinking and partying. Everyone that came up to him and said, "I thought you were going to stop drinking, or take it slow," or "I thought you were going to make your granny proud." He would say, "This is the last time, relax, or chill, don't worry. I'm just having fun on my last night of drinking." Most of the family was excited for him, and some even said, "Leave him alone, let him enjoy his last night drinking." He is with his family. He apologized to some of his cousins and aunts for drinking too much. Lil Reggie made it through the party and then left with some of his cousins to watch the fight. When he got to the fight party, he continued drinking, and eventually, he was drunk and had little control over his body and words. Lil Reggie came to his auntie's house in the middle of the night and was talking loud and acting up, so his aunt warned him that if he didn't calm down, she was going to call the police. Lil Reggie didn't calm down, so at about 3:30 AM, his aunt called the police and she told Lil Reggie that she called them, and he said he was leaving before the police came, and he left the house walking. The police never showed up, and they believed that the police had picked Lil Reggie up and put him in a drunk tank for walking down the streets intoxicated. At about 6:30 AM, one of his cousin said she got up to find out if Lil Reggie went outside to sleep in the van that was parked in the driveway because she thought she heard him get in the van when the commotion was going on. She also checked her aunt's garage, but he was nowhere to be found. His cousin couldn't believe that he had really left and said maybe the police did pick him up for being drunk, so she called the police station, and they didn't have anyone in custody. She started to worry about him, so she called the hospitals in the area. She got dressed and decided to drive around the neighborhood—no luck. She went over his father's ex-girlfriend's house—no luck. She went over to his uncle's house—no luck. She thought he might have had a few friends in the area, but the streets were blocked off; she started calling back to the house to just find out if anyone had heard from him or knew where he was sleeping off his drunkenness—no luck. His cousin said she drove around the city, and before she knew it, she was on the other side of town, still no luck.

Barbara was in Jamaica and her sister and her sister's granddaughter was staying at Barbara's house. It was likely that Lil Reggie would go home to Barbara's house, so Barbara's niece called the house to see her mother or her daughter had heard from Lil Reggie, no luck. Nothing she tied or did helped her find where Lil Reggie's had gone in the middle of the night, walking while he was intoxicated. He had to be in jail or over someone's house sleeping off the alcohol; she gave up her search, no luck.

Around 11:00 AM, there was a knock on Barbara's door, and her niece went to the door, sure that it was Lil Reggie at the door since they were looking for him and he always came home after he had a bout, regardless of what Barbara had told him. When she opened the door, there was a gentlemen at the door. He exchanged hellos and told her he was sorry to bother her, but he needed to ask her some questions. First question was if she was the only one in the house. She said, "No, my grandmother is here. She is in the shower." Then he asked her, "Do you know this person in this picture?" It was a copy of a driver's license. She answered, "Yes, that's my cousin, Reggie." The gentleman said, "I am very sorry to inform you, but he was found dead in Oakland this morning, and we need someone to come and identify his body."

She froze in her tracks, she could not move or speak, she let out a loud scream, "Naaannnnnnnnnaaaaaaaaaaaaaa." She just kept screaming. Her grandmother could feel the scream deep in her soul. She came running out of the bathroom, "What's wrong?" But she knew what kind of scream that was. She asked the question, but she knew that was a scream of loss. Her granddaughter just kept screaming. She looked at the gentlemen at the door, and all she could say was, "Who . . . who is it? Who is it? Tell me, who is it? Who . . . who is dead? Tell me! She knew the visit involved a notification of death;

she just didn't know whose death. Then her granddaughter answered for the gentlemen. She said, "It's Lil Reggie, Nana, it's Lil Reggie on the picture."

She just stared at the gentlemen and asked him if he was sure. She told him that she had just seen him last night. She asked him, "What happened to him?" The officer reported that he had been shot and that someone needed to come and identify the body, but the driver's license was found in his pocket. They were both crying and trying to get as much information as they could. Barbara's sister said all she could think about was her sister who was in Jamaica, and she had only been there for one day. How and who was going to tell Barbara that her grandbaby was dead. Her sister called all her other family members and told them the sad news, one by one. They all met at Barbara's house. It was one of the worst tragedies that the family had ever experienced. The same questions kept coming up over and over again, each one of them asked, "How are we going to break the news to Barbara? Who is going to tell her and when. They kept saying how she had just left and went on vacation, and how someone needed to be there with her when she was told. Barbara's sister that had received the notification was the one that was chosen to call Barbara. They planned to call the hotel and ask for Barbara's traveling companion first and tell her what had happened so she could stay in the room with Barbara. Barbara remembers that the hotel phone rang, and when she answered it, her sister was on the line and she asked Barbara if her traveling companion, Nicole, was in the room with her. Barbara said, "Yea, she's sitting right here," then Barbara asked her sister, "What you doing calling here on the hotel phone?" Her sister asked her, "Is Nicole close to you?" Barbara said, "Yea, she's sitting right here in front of me, what do you want? What's going on?"

Her sister asked to speak to Nicole, and Barbara asked her again, "What do you want with Nicole, what's going on?" Finally, Nicole said, "Give me the phone, she wants to speak to me." So Barbara just handed Nicole the phone; she remembered thinking, *What did she want with Nicole?* But she didn't make a big deal out of it because she was on vacation, and maybe her sister wanted to surprise her with a bottle of champagne or something special. Nicole answered the phone in a jovial and exciting tone. "Hello" in a Jamaican accent. She went on to say something fun about being in Jamaica, and then Barbara's sister told Nicole to hold on to her expression, but she had some sad news that she needed to tell Barbara. She went on to say, "This morning, Lil Reggie was killed, and we need to tell her." Nicole let out a gasp, and Barbara, who had started busying herself with something else in the room turned around and just looked at Nicole. She said, "What, what is it?" Barbara asked her again, "What did she say? What does she want?" Barbara's sister told Nicole, "Just stay in the room with her and hand her the phone." Nicole was holding her breath and just handed Barbara the phone, trying not to make eye contact. Barbara asked her sister again, "What do you want? What's going on? What are you doing call here for Nicole?" Her sister said, "I was calling for you." Barbara said, "Is my house all right?" Then her sister said, "I have some news about Lil Reggie," and before she could finish, Barbara said, "Oh Lord, what happened? What did he do now?"

Barbara said there was this long pause on the phone; it was a calm before the storm, she told Barbara, "Lil Reggie was killed this morning." Barbara said she doesn't remember anything that was said after that; she didn't know how, by whom, where, or when, they never got that far. She remembers feeling like someone had ripped her heart right out of her chest. Nicole said Barbara screamed so loud that everyone in the hotel could hear her, then she dropped the phone, and Nicole tried to console her, but there was nothing she could do or say, so she just let Barbara feel the emotion that had taken over her entire being, just felt helpless, so she just let her cry and cry and cry. Eventually, Nicole picked the phone up. Barbara's sister was responding to Barbara's pain and was no longer on the phone; she was being consoled by the family at Barbara's house, while Big Reggie held the phone waiting for someone to get back on the phone. Nicole said "hello" and then heard Big Reggie's voice; he told her they were going to get Barbara a ticket to come home, and they wanted her to keep an eye on Barbara. Nicole agreed and said she is taking it hard. Big Reggie said, "We all knew she would. We are glad you are there with her. He then told Nicole he would call back after the travel arrangements were made to give her the flight number. Barbara's sons worked out the details to get Barbara a ticket to come home; he thanked Nicole again.

Big Reggie had to identify his only child's body, which was the hardest thing he has ever had to do. He was in shock and hurt; he could imagine what happened that would make someone want to kill Lil Reggie. Barbara wasn't able to leave Jamaica for another two days; while her sons worked on getting her home, the morgue informed the family that even though Lil Reggie's biological mother and father were living, Lil Reggie's body could only be released to Barbara, which made her return home even more urgent. Barbara remembers questioning what she could have done differently, what she could have done that would have had a different outcome.

The details of Lil Reggie's death were unclear because it was an ongoing investigation and no information was released to the family. What Barbara and her family knew was Lil Reggie had been shot, and he ran from the area where he was shot, and at some point, he collapsed in the middle of the streets on an island that divides four lanes of traffic, two on each side. What Barbara and her family knew was that it was really early in the morning when the incident happened; they also knew that when his cousin was looking for him and the streets were blocked, it was because the police had taped off the streets where Lil Reggie was lying in the middle of the island where he had collapsed. It made sense to his cousin after she found out where the incident took place. Lil Reggie was predictable; he was going over his father's ex-girlfriend's house, just as his cousin had thought, but he never made it. The family also knew that it was not likely that Lil Reggie was killed by an enemy; they believed he had to be murdered by a stranger and the police agreed.

Barbara described her reaction to the news of her firstborn grandchild and the child she raised as her own as having an out-of-body experience. She questioned how this could be happening to her and her little baby boy; it was personal, and it was painful. Barbara's son offered to have his wife meet her in Jamaica to fly home with her so she wouldn't be alone for the ten-hour traveling time. Barbara said she didn't think it was necessary to have someone fly there to fly back with her; she said she would be okay and headed home. She said she doesn't really remember the trip home; it was uneventful. She remembers balling up in the corner against the window of the plane and every now and then sobbing for her baby boy. While she was flying home, she realized she had not asked much about what happened to Lil Reggie; her only real question was, "Are you sure it was him? Who would kill Lil Reggie and why? Why did they have to kill him? The most he would do was get drunk and start talking loud, but he was not violent. He wouldn't hurt a fly." Lil Reggie's death made no sense at all, and it was a terrible blow to the entire family.

When Barbara's plane finally landed, reality set in; she had to go to the morgue to have the body released to the funeral home. Barbara couldn't explain what it felt like to see her baby boy lying in a body bag. Imagine your worst heartbreak and multiply it by five, which only attempted to paint the picture of despair that she felt. As we all know, there are some experiences that we just don't have the ability to put into words. She said she couldn't talk, think, or move; the only thing she can do is moan and groan to get through her out-of-body experience. Thank God that the Holy Spirit interprets our moans and groans; the Lord has left us a helper who will comfort and carry us when we go through the indescribable painful experiences in life, and this was one of those times for Barbara.

After Barbara signed the papers to release Lil Reggie to the funeral home, her work was not done; she was responsible for making funeral arrangements for Lil Reggie, but her family didn't leave her alone. They were all by her side, including Lil Reggie's mother, to help with arrangements. Barbara was openly grieving, and she kept thinking if she were not on vacation and had attended the party that night, Lil Reggie would still be alive. People kept visiting her during the time when the family was making the arrangements so Barbara kept herself engaged in conversations with family and friends but said she did more listening than talking; many people came over and told light and funny stories about Lil Reggie and his life. Most everyone remembered the early days when Lil Reggie wanted to be a rapper and how he always wanted to dress nice and wanted to look good. One guy told the story that Lil Reggie had called him to come and pick him up late at night because he was out, and he said, "Come and get me, man. I have all of this money on me and I need a ride. I shouldn't be out here with all this money on me." So his friend agreed to pick him up, and when he asked him, "Why are you outside this time of night with lots of money on you?" He said that Lil Reggie just pointed to his clothes and said, "I got on Gucci and Prada." And his friend realized that he was referring to what he was wearing, and that is what he meant by "all this money on me." It was just one of many funny stories that people told about their friendship with Lil Reggie. The funeral was sad and full of young people in disbelief. People told upbeat stories, which was a reflection of Lil Reggie's personality. Others tried to encourage Barbara and the rest of the family, but offering themselves to them if they needed anything. At the end of the funeral, Barbara refused to let the funeral attendants close the casket; she kept asking, or should I say begging, "Please don't close it, please don't close it, please . . . ." It was one of the saddest ending of a funeral that was ever witnessed; she didn't want to say goodbye. She didn't want him to be alone; she didn't want it to be the final moment. After much crying and pulling and crying and negotiating, the attendants were finally about to close the casket; it was sad. Barbara doesn't remember who attended Lil Reggie's funeral; she knows there were many people there who gave her hugs and condolences. Some people told her to trust God and have faith. Barbara's remembrance of the funeral is mostly a series of stories that others have told her about the service and the day. Her grief rendered her in a trance state, like the elderly parent suffering from Alzheimer's; she cannot recall the complete story without struggle.

Barbara, unlike many mothers who have experienced the death of a child or loved one, was informed that the person who had shot Lil Reggie was caught and he admitted to shooting Lil Reggie, claiming that he was drunk and he thought he was going to hurt one of his friends. The young man also admitted he didn't know Lil Reggie, nor did he have an altercation that caused him to shoot him. Court proceedings have revealed that the shooter was a nineteen-year-old boy who was in a gang; he admitted that his friend told him later, after he had shot Lil Reggie, that Lil Reggie was asking for a light for his cigarette. He shot him in cold blood, and Lil Reggie started running. He chased him and shot him in the back. The murder trail took a toll on Barbara; every time they went to court, it was like living the whole incident all over again. Barbara recounts the anxiety and the questions she had about Lil Reggie dying senselessly. Barbara was full of "whys." Why had the boy in handcuffs across the room steal her grandson's life? Why did he shot him in the back? Why did he chase him? Why did he have a gun? Why did God let this happen? She also wanted to know what Lil Reggie's his last words were. She had so many questions. As time went on, the evidence revealed that Lil Reggie had done nothing but ask the boy's friend for a light for his cigarette. Lil Reggie also told the friend when he saw the gun that he meant him no harm. He held his hands in the air and started to walk away, but the boy shot him, first in the forearm and Lil Reggie started to run, then he shot him in the back. What a waste of life for both Lil Reggie and the boy. Eventually, the boy took a plea bargain that required him to spend the rest of his natural life in prison. Both families were in mourning; neither one was coming home again, and their mothers were heartbroken.

 Barbara says she misses Lil Reggie every day, and it is hard for her to go to the city where he was killed and especially the block where he laid in the middle of the streets. She has even had a hard time going to the church that she attended prior to the murder. Barbara shared that just sitting still in any normal place has been hard. She said some days are much harder than others; she knows that she is still grieving and often she imagines him in the middle of the streets and wonders what that experience of getting shot was like for him and if he was in a lot of pain. She wonders if someone could have saved him; she said her mind wonders and is full of thoughts and she mourns for him and often asked, "Why did he have to die and why did he have to die like that?"

 Barbara has had a hard time letting go of the idea that she could have possibly saved Lil Reggie from his fate. She questioned her actions and his outcome with the never-ending "if only," which implies that she had some control or responsibility in the death of Lil

Reggie. Could she have saved him from his own fate? Could she have prolonged his life? Questions that come out in the form of a statement, like what would have happened "if only" she had allowed him to stay in the house while she was gone on her vacation. She thought "if only" she had convinced Lil Reggie to stop drinking, he may still be alive. "If only" she didn't go on her vacation, she could have been there that night; she could have made sure he didn't leave the party. "If only" one of the other family members in the house would have stepped in and stopped him from leaving. "If only" she could have taken his place. Barbara was no stranger to the experience of death; she had lost several significant others in her lifetime, including her mother, grandmother, and two brothers; but this pain was like no other she had ever experienced. Her thoughts were invaded by the "if only" statements and questionings that are saturated in remorse and guilt about her relationship with Lil Reggie. Guilt and remorse can lead anyone down a road of unrealistic beliefs that they somehow had control over another person's fate. That belief not only can complicate the grieving process but also helps create a faulty remembrance about the life of the person and can even lead to mental illness for the person suffering from complicated grief.

Barbara's grieving process has been complicated because it is filled with so many things, including her regrets about her relationship with Lil Reggie and her beliefs that she somehow could have changed or controlled the outcome of his life and death. It's also complicated with her believe that God could have stepped in at any time to control the outcome, why didn't he. Barbara is pretty mad at God for not stepping in because she knows he ultimately controls everything. When our hearts are heavy, the last thing we want to hear is comments like "God is in control of everything" or "everything happens for a reason," "this too shall pass"; we know they mean well, but the truth is, the confusion and hurt is so great the words do very little to comfort us in the midst of grief. Those kinds of comments made Barbara question God even more and disrupts our faith as believers. God understands our questioning of Him and his plan; he is full of mercy and will give peace to those who are being bombarded with chaos. "*Let the peace that Christ gives control your think-*

ing, because you were all called together in on body to have peace. Always be thankful" (Colossians 3:15)*. He also tells us, *"I leave you peace; my peace I give you. I do not give it you as the world does. So, don't let your hearts be troubled or afraid" (John 14:27).*

He understands when we are confused and unable to understand those things that God allowed and shows us compassion even when we question him. *"Praise to the God of All Comfort, Praise be to the God and Father of our Lord Jesus Christ, the Father of compassion and the God of all comfort, who comforts us in all our troubles, so that we can comfort those in any trouble with the comfort we ourselves receive from God" (2 Corinthians 1:3–4).* After all, he came down to live among us in the flesh, and to die in front us in the physical, he knows the pain of life and death. Everything on earth "must die"; we all must die, but the good news is, we don't have to stay dead. God assures us that a relationship with him will help us take this life experience as a temporary training ground, an earthly boot camp, in preparation for an eternal resting place in heaven. We know we are all going to die, so why are we so surprised, upset, shocked when we experience the loss of a loved one, mostly because it's so final, or at least that is what we tell ourselves; it is true on earth, we will exist without the loved one, on earth it is forever, but God has offered us a new hope in a never-ending relationship with Him. This life is the stop in the train station, not the final destination of the journey. Barbara is still having a hard time with putting her complete hope in the all-knowing God because she knows, that He knew the outcome of the situation, and she knows He could have intervened if he wanted to. She is hurt and wants to know why didn't He want to intervene for Lil Reggie. She has so many "whys" and if "onlys" that it hurts to even think about.

We start the questioning ritual, asking God about death, His plan, and how he could allow tragedy, hurt, and destruction, because it all seems so harsh and in direct conflict of the loving God we serve. His love is indescribable, unmeasurable, and unduplicatable; how then could he allow such devastation? God warns us that he is not like us, his thoughts are not our thoughts, and his ways are not like our ways. God's decisions should not be measured or examined for living on this temporary training ground called earth, God's decisions, should be scrutinized as a part of his plan and preparation for us to live in eternity, which affects circumstances and situations on earth. If we lived in a world without devastation and tragedy, it's likely that very few people would turn from their wicked ways and serve God. A world with no consequences for actions or inactions is doomed to suffer human destruction. There would also be no need for God to step in or step aside.

Think back to a painful experience and consider the outcome after some time had passed; generally, we look back and say, "If that had not happened, I would not be where I am today," even in some of the most devastating situations. When we put our hope in God, no matter how painful our experiences are, he promises that he is working them out for the good of those who love him. God promises that through him we have gained access by faith into his grace, *"And we boast in the hope of the glory of God. Not only so, but we also glory in our sufferings, because we know that suffering produces perseverance; perseverance, character; and character, hope. And hope does not put us to shame, because God's love has been poured out into our hearts through the Holy Spirit, who has been given to us" (Romans 5:2–5, NIV).* We can stand on the promises of God, even the promise that in this life we will encounter suffering, but he also assures us that we can find peace in the midst of our trouble, in Him. He says, *"I have told you these things, so that in me you may find peace. In this world, you will have trouble, but take heart! I have overcome the world" (John 16:33, NIV).*

Our hope should rest in our understanding of heaven and what's to come because everything here is temporary; we must all die, but we don't have to stay dead! God is real, and so is heaven. He tried to help us better understand death, not only did he die so that we might live, and be reconciled to Him; he also demonstrated suffering of the righteous. No man's suffering could ever compare to the suffering that God experienced by his people and for his people. Barbara knows God offers her hope for tomorrow and what's to come after this life. She also knows she has to get to know God and his promises about what he has stored up for her in heaven. God gives us a "how to live" book but nothing in the book gives us a promise of how long we will live . . . . "If only."

Freewill vs God's Will
Meet Amanda

Amanda is a forty-one-year-old single woman and a twin, and she has one older brother, two younger sisters, and two younger brothers. Amanda's mother and father married very young and their marriage produced three children, her and her twin and her older brother who refers to her as "his big little sister." Amanda grew up in a city with a known repetition of violence and drugs; there was no resemblance of a city of angels. She remembers the city being filled with darkness and the unknown. Her home felt safe even though she watched her mother try to deal with sadness and sickness that was rooted in her own upbringing and her position in her family of origin. Amanda says it was difficult watching her mother try to deal with the unresolved hurts and sadness from her own childhood; her moods would swing, and there were days when she had highs, and they all enjoyed the comfort of a mother's love and happiness, but there were just as many lows where they witnessed their mother struggle with her sadness, which they referred to as Mommy's sickness. Amanda never saw her mother self-medicate her sadness, but she does remember referring to her mother's bouts of drug use as time when "Mommy is sick." And in spite of her mother's drug addiction, Amanda remembers her mother really trying to be a good mother, and how hard she struggled with stability and soberness. Amanda states that her mother was a "functioning addict" who made things happen for her children. With the help of Amanda's father, Amanda's mother was able to manage the responsibility of trying to raise her three children and get high, because Amanda's father was always present in all of his children's lives even after he and Amanda's mother were divorced.

For many years, Amanda's father and mother shared custody over their children until Amanda's "Mommy's sickness" took its toll on her ability to be present in her children's lives, leaving their father to provide as primary caregiver of them all. Amanda says by the time her and her twin turned eleven years old, her mother had become habitually sick, and it was at that time they went to live with their father on a permanently full-time basis. Amanda said the world with their mother was filled with sadness and sickness, but it was also filled with fun and love. She remembers always trying to save her mother; she would do anything to make her mother's sickness go away, regardless of what people would say, she believed she was all her mother had; she was her mother's only constant, and even though stepping in was filled with unfulfilled promise, disappointments, and worry, Amanda would always fight for her mother's life, even when her mother didn't fight for her own life. The therapeutic label that is placed on those that aide a person while they are at the center of their drug addiction is co-dependency, but to child caring for a drug-dependent parent, the label that best fits is "unconditional love" and that's what Amanda had, even if it only added to the sickness of her mother, she loved her past her sickness, and all her inabilities to keep her word. Amanda recounts that she would do anything for her mother and the best advice anyone could give her about the caring she provided for her "drug sick" mother was keep loving her because it was her only plan she had made for their relationship.

Amanda's mother was born in a family where the color of your skin allowed for certain benefits and privileges, which is familiar in many African American families. Amanda's mother was one of the "dark-skinned" children who received no favoritism; in fact, Amanda's grandmother showed an open disdain toward her "dark children," and each of them masked their childhood pain in some way or another. Amanda's mother married young, and when the pain became unbearable, she self-medicated with drugs and alcohol. Some of Amanda's mother's siblings also become drug dependent while others became self-destructive with lawlessness and violence. In fact, some of the "dark-skinned children" became notorious violent drug dealers, whose deeds are too harsh and illegal to recant in a titled book such as this. The therapeutic labels placed on many people with the type of behavior that act out and prey on people to mask their deep-rooted pain as a result of rejection and abandonment for unchangeable self attributes is often referred to as "self-hatred" and for a child and often leads to destruction of self and others. Amanda's grandmother had created a mess that she could not deny simply by rejecting her children and denying them of the type of love they should have been entitled to, had it not been for the color of their skin.

Amanda and her siblings noticed how bad her grandmother treated their mother, and thought it must have been because their mother was sick. Amanda reflected on a story about her grandmother where she would buy all the light-skinned grandchildren lavish gifts for Christmas and she and her siblings would get almost nothing, but they were required to watch the other kids play with their gifts from "nanny" who was loving and kind to them. Amanda wondered what she and siblings had done wrong that would make them be subjected to such unfavorable treatment. Amanda questioned, "Why would nanny love them more than us?" One would have thought it was Amanda and her siblings that really needed the most love and attention; after all, their mother was the one sick, but "nanny" must not have seen it the same way as her grandchildren did.

By the time Amanda turned seventeen, her mother was sick and tired of being sick and tired and got clean and sober almost on her own. Amanda remembers it being a really good time, almost too good to be true. She spent that one year while her mother was in recovery getting to know her mother better and the source of her deeply rooted pain. Amanda's mother had returned to her wellness and was no longer labeled as sick. Amanda explained that her mother joined church and even got married to a man that Amanda believed was good for her mother. They began to build their life together, and her mother made it a point to include her children in the new life, even though they were nearly adults. Amanda remembers watching her mother closely, mostly out of fear; she didn't want her mother to go back to her old life that was filled with sickness and drugs. Amanda kept in touch with her mother almost every day, some checking out of excitement and love, and some checking out of fear and concerned; all she wanted her mother to do is stay clean and sober, which translated to stay "well." The relationship between Amanda and her mother grew strong and close, and they enjoyed each other. Her mother was on a new journey in life; she joined a church, got baptized, moved into a really nice place. She was a grandmother and being clean and sober gave her the opportunity to be more accountable with her eldest son's child than she had been with her own children. Amanda remembers her mother showing up and keeping promises, playing a significant role in her children's lives as well as her granddaughter's life. Amanda was most impressed with how attentive and loving her mother was to her granddaughter, and although they all agreed to share in the upbringing of the granddaughter, her mother was taking the lead.

Amanda's mother stayed clean and sober for over a year. Amanda remembers calling her mother and not talking to her mother but didn't think much of it. She wasn't sure the exact date of her mother's relapse, but she remembers that her mother started avoiding her and making excuses again about when, where, and how, which was the red flag for Amanda. She knew it was too good to be true. Only this time, her mother was not only using again, but she and her new husband had also started dealing drugs, which added even more complications to the accountability of her whereabouts and the trust that Amanda had on the reliability of her mother's promises. Amanda knew that her mother had a love hold on her, and she would more often than not give in to her mother and her false promises of the future for a treasured moment of the right now. Seeing her mother happy and smile, even if it was just to get what she wanted and using her to feed her habit or for assurance that someone loved her, more than she loved herself. Amanda recalls this time was different; she was angry at her mother because she had the opportunity to witness her mother "well," and she learned that there was a cure for her mother's "sickness," and it was inextricably tied to her being clean and sober. Amanda was hurt; when she was growing up, she gave her mother unconditional love and her mother's excuses made sense to her growing up even if they were filled with disappointments because they were tied to her sickness. But Amanda realized that even her love for her mother had conditions; there is a cure for your sickness, and she needed her mother to make some choices. Choice for her children and her granddaughter. Amanda's mother really had no idea that her clean and soberness was tied to the hopes and dreams of children who had an experience of love filled with disappointments from unkept promises and gentle bites of sickness that were equivalent to a child's overeating of sweets and treats, basically an unexplained stomachache that could turn into a series of unexplained other sicknesses if untreated as time went on. Her children longed for the reliability of their mother's presences and promise, and they knew that her relapse was a relapse for all of them. What's worst is her sickness was unfamiliar to her granddaughter; she only knew the reliably "well" grandmother, but for her children, "Mommy was sick again." Amanda was so upset with her mother; she felt like her mother traded in her love for her children in exchange for her addiction. She had never questioned her mother's love or abilities before, but things had changed and so had Summer. After Amanda's mother started her sickness ritual of unreliability and inconsistency again, Amanda began to feel some resentment and anger toward her mother because her mother had also started disappointing her granddaughter by showing up really late or not showing up at all.

Amanda tells the story that one day she and her niece were waiting for her mother because it was her mother's turn to watch her niece, but the agreed-upon time had long passed and Amanda had given up on her mother, but she didn't want her niece to take notice of the unkept promise of her grandmother. When Amanda's mother did show up to take her granddaughter, Amanda would not let her mother take her granddaughter. Amanda was so upset, she gave her mother a lecture and told her that she needed to get clean and sober again before she could be trusted to with her granddaughter or their feelings. Amanda remembers her mother pleading with her to take her granddaughter with her; she promised to bring her back on time. She promised to take good care of her, but Amanda received her mother's request as just another con to get what she wanted, like the old days. Amanda knew in the past she would give into her mother's pleading, but Amanda said this time it was different. She was not going to let her mother take advantage of her, so no matter how much her mother pleaded and hugged and kissed her, Amanda refused to give into her mother's request to take her granddaughter with her. Amanda remembers feeling real strong, mostly out of hurt and disappointment, but regardless, she was not going to give in, and no matter how much her mother pleaded, Amanda stuck to her "no," which had not happened in the past. Amanda said she was angry with her mother because her niece never knew the grandmother with the broken promises. She only knew the loving, kind grandmother who was accountable and reliable. Eventually, Amanda's mother left, and Amanda felt sad and good at the same time, sad that her mother was back to her old bad habits and good that she had stuck to her "no" and did not allow her love for her mother to cloud her judgment.

Amanda understood her mother's sickness and that it had caused her not be dependable or reliable; Amanda also understood her mother's pain and the fact that her mother used drugs to medicate her sickness and pain to deal with the experiences saturated with adversities from her upbringing, but what Amanda understood most was her mother's love, which is why Amanda always gave into her mother and vowed never to turn her back on her mother, so saying no and holding her ground was so hard to do. Amanda's good feeling of standing up to her mother was short-lived. Some time in the middle of the night, Amanda was woken by a phone call where the caller on the other end had a piercing scream, and Amanda just heard that she had to come to what was known as a safe place for their family. It was a direct order, so Amanda and her niece did as she was instructed; it was Amanda's grandmother on the other end of the call, and she refused to tell Amanda who was behind the reason for the demand to get to the safe house. Amanda recalls that when she got there, everyone in the family was crying and she asked over and over again what's happened, what's wrong. Amanda was no stranger to death; even at eighteen years old, her family had lost lives, and they had also been accused of lives lost. Amanda recalls it was her uncle who looked her in the eye and said, "It's your mother and Lenard. They have been killed." Amanda says she didn't hear much more than that; she could feel sorrow, guilt, and pain collide, and it was the beginning to a battle deep in her mind and soul. "How could this be? I just saw her, I just talked to her." Amanda admits she was in denial and disbelief; her mother could not be dead, she and her mother had just started a new track on how to relate that was going to help them both change their ritual behavior of Amanda giving in to her mother; she had never said "no" to her mother. How could it be that the one time she said "no" would be the last time she would see her mother and the last thing she would say to her mother, how could this be? The report was that her mother was shot seventeen times and Lenard was shot twelve times in a drive-by shooting and her mother's last words were a message of love to her kids. Amanda was devastated to say the least; she remembers being heartbroken. She wanted revenge, she wanted street justice, she wanted to die too, she wanted her "mama" back. She would cry for hours, but *God's promises that "those who sow with tears will reap with songs of joy" (Psalm 126:5, NIV)*. Just wait on him.

Amanda has some really good memories of her mother's love, despite her mother's choices. Amanda remembers going into a downward spiral and her mind and soul begin an internal battle that took over her body and for the first five years of her mother's death; she started going down the same destructive path as her mother. Amanda said she started getting high, drinking, being undependable, unreliable, lying, and anything else she could do that required unacceptable rebellious behavior that did not honor her mother's memory.

Amanda remembers being suicidal and wanting to take her own life. Life had started to become unmanageable, and she just didn't want to play anymore. Amanda said she had thought about suicide many times but never followed through, mostly because of her close relationship with her brother, her twin sister, and her niece who had all been through enough hurt and pain in their lives, and she didn't want to be the cause them experiencing even more pain. Amanda said her family was her only reason for living, but it was all becoming too much for her and she carefully devised a plan to take herself out of her misery, the misery she created herself with her faulty thinking and the labels she was wearing about her and her life. So she wrote letters to each one of her family members, letting them know how sorry she was about her decision to leave this earth. She spent the day with her twin sister, said her goodbyes, and drove to the pier to complete the suicide. She sat in her car drinking and reminiscing about her childhood, her family, and her memories of her mother and her mother's death. She knew that she had spent a lot of time blaming herself about things she didn't have control over. As she sat in her car, she remembered her mother's funeral and how sad they all were. She remembered how much she cried for her mother and then she started to cry; she was crying so hard that it was as if the years of her mother's death had not passed. She was there again; this time for her family, because she knew that the same thing would happen at her own funeral. She realized that she had started the process of mourning her own death, for her family, for her friends, and for herself. She knew that the whole ordeal would leave them as wounded as she was about her mother's death. How could she be so selfish? How could she do this to them? She sat in the car and cried and cried until she dosed off; suddenly there was a knock on her car window. It startled her. She jumped, and when her eyes came into focus, she realized it was the police. The police leaned toward the window and asked her to roll her window down; she had to turn the car on to roll the window down. When the window was rolled halfway down, she answered, "Yes." The officer asked her if she was okay; again she answered, "Yes." He asked her what was she doing there and told her that she couldn't just park there; he then told her it's 3:30 AM, and it was dangerous for a woman to be sleeping in her car on the pier alone. She said she must have just dozed off, and she would be leaving. He asked her for some identification, and then asked her if everything was all right again. It was just something in the way he said it that she knew he was a caring person. She could barely clear her throat; she confessed that life had taken its toll and she really didn't know what to do with all her feelings. He held her license in his hand for a while then he said, "Do you have someone in your family that could come and get you?"

She said, "No, I'm fine to drive. I just came out here to think." As she told him that horrible lie, tears started coming down again. The officer asked her again if she was all right, and then he told her he didn't want to just leave her to drive while she was so upset. He asked her about her parents; she told him that her mother had died some time ago and her father was probably asleep, and she hadn't talked to him in a few months. She said, "I will be all right, I just got a lot going on." He asked her for her father's number; she hesitated and said, "I don't want him involved in my pain and I couldn't call him. He has a new family and he would just worry."

The officer said, "Well, is there someone else I can call? I don't want to just leave you to drive. You are going to have to give me someone's number, because I'm not able to leave you in your own care." Just as the officer told Amanda her fate, another police car pulled up, and two officers got out of the car. They walked up to the officer who was still holding Amanda's driver's license, the officers greeted the officer and then looked into the car, and the officer introduced the other two officers to Amanda. Amanda said she became uncomfortable and asked if she was going to be arrested. The officer told her she was not in any legal trouble, but he believed she was in some emotional trouble and he couldn't just leave her in her emotional state in good conscious. One of the officers was a female; she asked Amanda to step out of the car. She asked again, "Am I being arrested?" She told her no. "It will help us talk to you without bending over into the car." Amanda stepped out of the car, and the female officer said, "My name is Brenda, and I have served this area for about five years, and sometimes we find people at this pier who are in despair, and we talk to them. On occasion, I have even prayed with some, other times we get here, and we find that people have desperate choice to relieve themselves of whatever pain they are in. Either way, we have to make a call to a family member, so what we are asking you is to help us made what we refer to as a 'good call.'"

Amanda looked at her and asked her to call her twin; she gave her the number and said her twin didn't live very far. While the officer was calling Amanda's twin, Brenda started talking to her; she told her that God was a healer. She asked her if she believed that. Amanda said she did and told her that she used to go to church all the time with her family. Brenda asked her what church they attended when she was growing up. Amanda told her and the name of the pastor. Brenda told her the name of the church she attended; she also told her, "We are told that we shouldn't mix church and state, but I believe that if it wasn't for God, we couldn't do our job safely, so I always let people know that the Lord is keeping me safe out here in the streets, especially in the middle of the night. I hope whatever you are going through that you know that you can get through it." Amanda was embarrassed and she was so uncomfortable knowing her twin was on her way. All three of the officers said some encouraging words of hope to her. All of them had a relationship with God and wanted her to know that they were human. When Amanda's twin finally made it, she jumped out of the car, crying, "Are you all right?" She grabbed Amanda and hugged her so tight. She said, "I knew something was wrong. I couldn't sleep. I kept thinking I wasn't ever going to see you again. What are you doing here? I thought you were going out of town." She grabbed her again and just hugged her; the officers said, "We are going to leave her with you. You can leave her car here until daylight, she won't get a ticket." As Amanda prepared to get in the car with her sister, Brenda gave her a card and invited them both to her church. She told them that even police officers have to cry sometimes, but God's promises that *"those who sow with tears will reap with songs of joy" (Psalm 126:5, NIV)*. Just ask him for what you need and wait on him. She also told them to come and check out the church, "I sing in the choir. There are a young people in your age group at the church." Amanda thanked them all and hugged Brenda; she was extremely grateful that the officer showed up and how kind the three of them were, but she was especially grateful to Brenda.

    Amanda didn't have the heart to tell her sister why she was at the pier to do that night; she has always made light out of it as if she was just getting high, and she fell asleep waiting on one of her friends who must have been scared off by the police. Her twin told her that they should go and visit the church that Brenda invited them to. Amanda agreed and one Sunday they got dressed up and went to the church. Brenda was excited to see them; she remembered Amanda and her twin right away. She was right; the church has a large young adult ministry, and Amanda and her twin fit right in. Amanda said she would just go because she was grateful that they help her in her hopeless state, but she wasn't really ready to commit fully to God, but she kept coming back, and the more she went, the more she learned, and the more God changed her and her heart. Amanda started going to Bible study, and she began to grow and heal. She still has bouts of sadness and even depression at times, but she knows that God has a plan for her life. Brenda and Amanda have become good friends over the years. Brenda never asked her about that night or if she was there to commit suicide; she just knew she was in trouble. Amanda has offered her testimony to others. She has said that her pain has become her ministry. God can use your storm to encourage others and give them hope for their situation. How many times have we heard someone say, "If you can make it through that, I know I'm going to be all right." God has used Amanda's situation many times to give hope to people who are struggling with grief, guilt, hurt, and forgiveness.

Amanda has forgiven the people who killed her mother that night and she has made peace with God, by the peace from God. She has made her life's mission to treat people with respect and kindness, the same type of kindness that Brenda and the other officers showed her on that dark night at the pier. Today, Amanda is a very responsible woman, who is on her way to becoming a doctor, but she takes no credit for her victories over life; she takes everything to God in prayer and allow God's word to lead her in her decisions. She is more than a conqueror. Amanda highly recommended that if you are struggling with the questions of why, and you want some answers to your experience of grief and justice, read *Why Do Bad Things Happen to Good People* by David Arnold and don't forget to read the Holy Bible, God's manual for living.

Why Did This Happen To Us
Meet Teena

Teena is a fifty-three-year-old mother of two boys. Her sons are thirty-two and twenty-four years old and her thirty-two-year-old has a three-year-old son. She grew up in Oakland, California, and is the third child of her mother's five girls. Teena tells the story of her mother having rules that each one of her girls had to abide by; she described her mother as being strict on her girls, not allowing them just hang out and do whatever they wanted to. Their mother was also well known in the neighborhood and had a reputation of being a very good cook, and she was known in the neighborhood to feed people who would stop by for a visit, which turned out to be often and also made her house the place where most kids in the neighborhood hung out.

Teena is a humble person with a quiet demeanor, at least at first glance; most people say she is so quiet, she hardly says anything, but this author begs to differ. Teena can be very vague and cautious in her interactions sometimes, but she has a lot to say about life and her experiences. In fact, this author credits some of the long in-depth conversations with Teena as being the reason for studying the subject of grief and going into a doctorate program to further my education. At the time of my own contemplation of furthering my studies, Teena's mother was battling cancer, and we would talk about grief and loss often to the point that we both wanted to know more. Just as everyone at some point has gotten the call that a life has ended, so too did this author, when Teena informed me that her mother's battle with cancer was over. I remember being so sad for the family, and I knew that each one of her girls would have a different response, but I also knew that all of them were hurting. *Who will cook for the cook?* I kept thinking. She had fed so many people, and as expected, so many people came to pay their respects to her life and mourned her leaving. I can still see their faces, all of them, her girls, her grandchildren, and even others who had grown up in their house; the mother of the neighborhood had died, and it was a sad day indeed. What does one say? "It will be all right. We all have to go through it"? What do you say? I chose to say, "If you need anything, let me know." It is a standard line that I have vacated from my vocabulary. First of all, I realized, whatever they needed at that time, it was most likely that I didn't have it or could not supply it to any of them; it's just a line that we use out of habit, ritual, trying to be kind, in a heavy situation. What I should have said was, "I have no idea what you are feeling, but if you need to talk, please feel free to call me" because that is something I could have provided for her, a listening ear, but not much else.

Teena and her family grieved the death of her mother, and it seemed to bring the girls even closer; their common, shared interest of caring for their mother was over, but their mourning her life had just started. Teena tells the story of her living in the same neighborhood as her children's father. She met him when she was sixteen years old, and he was seventeen years old. They lived fairly close to one another and took every opportunity to see each other every day. They were childhood sweethearts, and eventually Teena became pregnant and gave birth to her oldest son. Teena explains that after her child was born, her and the father broke up but still communicated with each other regarding issues concerning their son. Teena and her then boyfriend broke up for about one year; they decided to get married when their son was five years old. They had a small ceremony with just their siblings and parents; her mother walked her down the aisle, and after about eight years, they had another son. Teena and her husband lived a modest life; he was a postal worker and she also worked for the government. Their relationship started in childhood, so each of them brought some childish things to the marriage, but they made it through.

    Teena tells the story of getting a heart-wrenching phone call that her father-in-law had passed away. It affected the entire family dearly; he was not sick, no diseases, no diagnoses. He just passed away without warning. Teena thinks back to her father-in-law's death and remembers her husband was sad; he grew up in a house with two parents, but he didn't seem to display any public grief or mourning for the death of his dad, but she knew he was sad. She also started to notice some small changes in her husband's behavior, particularly as it related to trust. He started talking a lot about how he was being treated at work and how some people were responding to him; he eventually filed a discrimination complaint against his employer for harassment. Teena said his stories about the harassment got progressively worst and concerning, because some things didn't seem to add up, particularly that his employer was spying on him, and there was some conspiring against him. He started showing signs of being highly stressed and in need of some emotional help. At some point, the stress caused him to start seeing a therapist, who eventually diagnosed him with being delusional and paranoid. Teena believes that her father-in-law's death served as the trigger for her husband's full-blown diagnoses and caused interferences in his normal daily functioning. He started to withdraw from the relationship, and for that matter, many of his relationships. The more time passed, the worst the relationship between him and Teena got; they started having repetitive arguments. Teena didn't know what was going on because the treating psychologist never shared the diagnoses with Teena nor did her husband; she just thought he was stressed from his experiences at work, which made him become withdrawn. Teena repeatedly asked him to go to marriage counseling, and until he saw her taking steps to leave the relationship, he refused to go. At some point, they did start seeing someone, but it was short-lived, because he didn't trust the therapist or what was being said in therapy. Eventually, Teena and the boys moved out, and once they moved out, her husband agreed to start seeing someone on a regular basis. They had started dating again and making date nights, but Teena noticed that her husband had started taping the windows in the house, doing strange things that suggested that there was something else going on beside stress, and she became concerned but didn't want to suggest that her husband was having some kind of mental impairment or breakdown; it was just not talked about in many Black families—it's taboo. The most you might hear is "so and so is just going through it right now" as if "it" is common and we all have an "it" to go through at some point. It's not until the person has an actual psychotic break in many black families is there even a family discussion about the behavior. Furthermore, to suggest that the person needs treatment at the onset of a change in behavior is often received as betrayal by at least one family member, e.g. child, parent, spouse; they daresay or believe that the person they once knew is in a permanent state of mental change. Teena and her family were no different; she daresay that the nice, strong, vibrant man, who was the father of her children, the loyal loving son and brother of his birth family was exhibiting some mental paralysis, it would have been disloyal to him, his abilities, his family, and his manhood, so she kept those questionable behaviors to herself, to her house.

Teena explained that she never thought her husband was a threat or his behavior was questionable to the point that it caused her to fear for her or her children's life. Teena's youngest son, who was ten years old, was considered a "daddy's boy" and even though he, his mother, and his brother had moved out, he would still spend weekends with his father. He had started to recognize the changes in his father's behavior, particularly the fact that his father taped up all the window coverings so no light would come into the house, and that he claimed it was for privacy. He also noticed that from time to time, his father would blurt out things that had no real meaning to what was going on at the time. Her ten-year-old also began to comment that "Daddy is sick," but his daddy was still loving and kind to him and appeared to pose no threat to him. So when he asked his mother if he could go and spend the weekend with his daddy, his mother answered yes. Teena had talked to his dad a few days before the weekend, and it was all set. Teena said her son and his father was looking forward to their weekend, and the night before, she called his father to confirm that she was bringing him over in the morning, but he didn't answer. She thought it was odd, but she just went to bed. The next morning, she called him again and still no answer, so her and her son went to his house and knocked on the door, and still no answer. She remembered becoming concerned, because this was not normal behavior for her husband. She said she thought maybe he went out of town and didn't say anything, but she knew that he and his son was looking forward to their weekend. She said she got back into the car and called his mother, who said she had spoken to her son a couple of days ago, and it was just a normal conversation and he had not mentioned going out of town. She asked his neighbor if he had seen him and the neighbor said he had not seen him. Teena and her son drove to a nearby parking lot and called him again, and just and she was headed back, she received a call from her neighbor who told her that the police were there at the house. He also told her that her husband was in the house, and that he had passed away. Teena didn't remember the exact order of the details; what she remembered is calling his mother back and informing her that they had to meet at the house. The whole family met at the house and were informed by the police that it looked like a possible homicide had taken place. Teena's oldest son had been told that someone had killed his father, which added more turbulence to the family's experience. By the time he arrived at the house, the police had withdrawn their suspicion of a possible homicide and determined based on the environment and the weapon, it was more likely that it was a suicide. It was a tragedy; her husband had shot himself by inserting the gun in his mouth and the bullet went through his head. It was also determined that he had probably been deceased for a few days, and although his eldest son remembers his father asking him to take him to purchase a gun sometime earlier, there were always guns in the house, so no one in the family saw this coming; everyone remembered their last conversation with him as being normal.

    Teena remembers being in shock; it was like having an out-of-body experience. Her thoughts and pain had to be put aside for what she termed as "busy work." Her brain kept telling her to get it together. You have to take care of things, you have to make funeral arrangements, lay him to rest, make decisions, were, when, how, what, contact people, insurance, probate, mortgage, rent, her children's grief, her husband's family's grief, their questions, their input, she describes it as just, busy, busy, busy, no time to focus on her own loss, no mourning for her, no time to regret, reflect, would haves, should haves, no time to sleep, eat, drink, or think. Her life was disrupted and in full-blown turbulence. She felt like she should have followed the instruction most often given on an airline when they instruct all passenger, in the event of an emergency, and the need for oxygen, be sure to put your mask on first before attempting to help someone else. Teena was traveling with her two sons in this emergency life experience, and they both were grief-stricken, but she had violated the rules of attending to yourself first and was attending to others first, which caused her not to put her mask on at all.

Her youngest son needed to be with her every minute of the day, which further complicated her ability to attend to her own needs and take care of the business that needed to be handled concerning her husband's services. Teena became worried about his youngest son because he started to appear to have separation anxiety immediately. He would follow her throughout the house, stand outside the bathroom, ask her where she was going, even if it was just to the next room, yet she still did not have on a mask of any kind. On those rare occasions that she felt the sadness was overwhelming and she attempted to be in the moment with her grief, her sons could not take seeing their mother grieve and would say things like, "Come on, Mom," and she didn't want her sadness to impact them because they had already lost their father so she would just "suck it up." She just didn't get to cry or mourn; she just couldn't be in the moment to feel or deal with her own grief. She had to stay busy doing what she was supposed to do, what she had to do. Teena explained that the busy work and attending to others and not yourself has "side effects" including major depression, anxiety, and in other ways that she has yet to share with others. She has a relationship with God and even though she didn't question God's will, she did question herself. The separation was supposed to make their relationship better; it was supposed to help them appreciate each other and their family.

UNEXPECTED TURBULENCE

It was supposed to give them a break so that they could heal from the tension of their relationship. He was not supposed to die; death is final. Now all of her family fantasies were over and that cannot be reconciled. Teena recommends that when you experience unexpected turbulence in your own life, put your mask on first, and if you need to mourn publicly, do it, reach out to others, accept offers of help, but first and foremost, reach out to God; he will comfort you in your time of need. He will assure you, you can get through this, and he will heal your hurts and your family.

Where Were You God? Meet Nick and Nina

Meet Nick, who grew up with an advantage that most people will never experience. His father was wealthy, mostly because his father's—father's hard work paid off. They were a family that had generational wealth from what started as a family vineyard and grew to one of the largest international wine manufacturing companies. Nick knows he has lived a privileged life; he always considered himself as a generous person. He and his company have several programs to help underprivileged youth and families; without question, they give back.

Nick was married to Nina, who was five years younger than him. Her upbringing was quite different than Nick's; her mother and father were working class, first-generation Americans whose parents had come to the United States from London, England, and even though her family had a history in the wine industry, she recalls it was as consumers, not entrepreneurs. In fact, Nina says it was not a day that went by that her family set at the dinner table without wine or some sort of alcoholic beverage. It was as if the family dinner centered around the wine rather than food. Nina remembers being left at friend's house waiting for her mother to pick her up and times when her and her older brother were left siting outside waiting for her mother to come home. Nina says she believed that her mother's alcohol use was the causes of many family gatherings going wrong and even though her mother was never referred to as an alcoholic, her mother did come to grips with the fact that alcohol interfered with her life's daily functioning. Nina says by the time she was twenty-one years old, her mother had stopped drinking completely and learned to manage her life and life choices. It wasn't until Nina was in her late thirties that she realized that her mother had spent some time in a in-house treatment facility for alcoholism; it was ironic that she would meet and marry someone in the "alcohol business."

Nick and Nina had been married for over thirty years; it is the first and only marriage for them both. God blessed them with four children starting with Nick Jr. who was as serious as his father at a young age about business. Nick Jr. spent most of his childhood working at one of the local wineries and learning what his father did from day to day. David, who was the second born, was much into sports and rarely requested to work in the family business; he played every sport the school had to offer, and on those times when he was not playing on a team, he was watching some time in person or on television. David had the vision to become a professional athlete, and regardless of what his mother and father's vision was for him, he had his own mind. Nick said the doctor had told them they could expect another boy, and so as they busied themselves getting ready for a boy, they were shocked and surprised by their third child's arrival, which was a girl, whom they had planned on calling Julian, but as a result of the outcome, they made some major adjustments in their thinking, as well as their decorum, but the name change was simple; they named her Julianna. Julianna was the biggest surprise in Nick and Nina's life; both of them grew up with brothers and neither of them had sisters, so they assumed it would carry on in their lives as well, especially after being informed that they were having another boy. Nick and Nina raised their three children on a set of values that were heavy weighted in treating people right, with respect and carrying about your fellow man.

Nick admits that he nor his family attended church on a regular basis; they were spiritual but not religious. They knew that God was in control of the universe and protected them from danger, but they were busy and their lives didn't have much room for routine active worship. They had businesses all around the country and two in Europe. Nick and his two brothers were the sole owners of the businesses after the passing of their father who left everything to their mother, who eventually passed away too. Nick believes in the concept of "work hard, play harder," so every chance he got, he tended to take advantage of his opportunity to play. The family had an annual trip to Europe that they took with his two brothers and their families and his wife and kids. Their trip was an annual event that was as exciting as Christmas and Thanksgiving, in all there was at least Nick's oldest brother had two girls, his younger brother had one boy, all three were close in age to Nick and Nina's kids. By the time Julianna was about eight, Nina found out she was pregnant again, and although it was a blessing, her and Nick had thought they were done having children. Nina gave birth to one more child name Martin, who was the love of everyone's life. Martin was such a loving child; he reminded them all what life was really about. Nina was pregnant with Martin during the planned annual trip to Europe and decided she would not go, and no matter how much Nick tried to convinced her to attend, she declined. That one and only time was the only time the entire family was not together for the annual trip to Europe. As time went on, the trip never changed, but the number of people included begin to grow. First Nick Jr. added an addition, and then another, his own wife and daughters. Later, David would get married and eventually he had a son. Nick's brother's Edward and Daniel both had children around the same age as Nick's children. By the time, Martin was nineteen years old, the family had taken this trip countless of times, and they all seemed to equally love getting together and catching up on each other's lives. Each had taken some part of the family business and enjoyed the lifestyle that it afforded them, including cars, trips, boats, trust funds, limousine rides, and Nick's middle son, David, had recently invested in a major-league basketball team.

 Nick tells the story of June 15, 2009, when everyone was getting ready for the annual trip, it seemed more exciting than ever; Martin had graduated high school and had convinced his mother to allow him to bring his girlfriend, whom he had dated in high school. Martin's mother was apprehensive and didn't want to be responsible for someone's child nor did she want her son to think that she would ever approve of him having any type of relations with the underage minor. Martin always knew what to say to his mother to get her to go alone with his ideas and plans. He promised his mother that he and his girlfriend would fly with her and his dad on their private plane, and they would not do anything that would disrespect the family or themselves. Martin didn't let up, and at one point, he even threatened to stay home if she couldn't go. His mother was having a hard time with the request, but eventually she gave in. Martin was so happy; he gave his mother lots of hugs and kisses and thanked her for trusting him; he promised that he wouldn't let her down and she would not have any regrets.

After Nick Jr. had taken the position of CFO for the company, he and his dad had always flown together to discuss business because as much as the trip was for pleasure, they financially justified the trip by conducting business with their London-based offices. When Nina told Nick that Martin and his girlfriend were going and they were flying with them, Nick was surprised by the change of the routine arrangements, and he was surprised that his wife had not discussed the changes with him. Nick said he had learned from being married for all these years that it was not worth making a fuss over, so he just agreed that Martin and his girlfriend would fly with them. When Nick Jr. and his father started to discuss some of the issues that the businesses in London were having, it became clear that they needed to spend some time together to discuss the particulars, and they needed to include Nick, Julianna, and Nick's older brother, Edward, who was named as the CEO; it just made sense to use the twelve-hour fight to come up with a plan to discuss with the executive time in London. Nick discussed the need to rearrange the flight details with Nina and Nina suggested she fly with the others, but Nick was not having that; he was adamant that he and Nina fly together. It was settled; Nick, Nina, Nick Jr., his wife, Caroline, Julianna, her husband Fred, their three-year-old, Alexis, and Edward would fly together in the family's private plane. Nick also chartered another plane to accommodate ten of the family members, which included, Martin, his girlfriend Olivia, David, his wife Maria, their sons Ethan and Andrew, and Nick's younger brother Daniel, his girlfriend Alison (after getting a divorced), and his son Frank, from his first wife. Edward's wife Isabella, his two daughters, Jessica and Amber, Nick Jr.'s two daughters, Sophia and Christina were all flying commercial to go on their annual shopping extravaganza in Paris as they had done many times before. Other family members had different plans, but they were all flying commercial and flying in on different times and days.

As they sealed their final travel plans about the week and plans to try something different, Nick said he remembered thinking that Martin had pulled a fast one, and he was unsure how he got away with bringing a girlfriend, when all the other kids had never been allowed. He remembered thinking that he was going to be watching their every move because he didn't want her to get pregnant or for anything else to happen while she was with their family. He also remembers hearing Nick Jr. present the issues and the proposals for the London operations, but he was unable to focus, and at one point, Nick Jr. asked him, "Are you listening?" He had to admit that he wasn't, so they all agreed to take a break to clear their minds. They are started having general conversation and Martin's name came up, and Nick Jr. took the opportunity to say, "I was surprised you all agreed to let his girlfriend come. You guys never let us bring anyone that wasn't family on this trip." Nina said, "You're right, I guess I have changed or the times have changed, but I'm going to be watching them both and they are sleeping in separate rooms. I don't care what he says." They remember laughing really hard about how Martin always is able to convince them that they are behind the times and everybody does this or that. After about three hours, they resumed their business discussions and came up with the much-needed plan for the London executives.

Once they all got settled in the house, Nina met with Martin and Olivia to lay down the house rules, so they could be clear that she and Nick were not going to stand for any disrespect while they were on the trip. Martin and Olivia agreed that they were there to follow the family rules and understood that they would not be sharing a room. Nina informed them of the sleeping arrangements and that Martin would be sharing a room with Ethan, Andrew, and Frank and Olivia would be sharing with all the other single women in the house. Nina said she loved the way Martin's girlfriend responded to her; she was a well-raised girl, and Nina knew she was sincere that nothing disrespectful was going to happen. Olivia said she was just glad to be on the trip that she had heard so much about over the years. Nina said everyone got alone good, and even though the other family members gave Olivia a hard time for being the first underage girlfriend to go, they laughed and had one of the best trips they had ever had. Nina said she knew her parenting focus had changed when Martin came along; she loved when he was happy, and she could see that he was extremely happy around Olivia, and Nina was happy that Olivia had taken the trip with the family. Martin was so happy and Nina could see how much he had grown up and how mature he behaved around Olivia; it reminded her of her and Nick. They had a real friendship and seemed to love each other. New relationships were formed, and the family had eaten together and reminisced as they had done for years. Nick remembered thinking that he was the cause of these people being together; it was a proud feeling of "look at what I created and was responsible for"; he said he knew his own father would have been proud to know how far they had took the business and how well they got along.

When it was time to leave, Nina suggested that they all go home the same way they came. Edward said he didn't mind taking the charter with his other brother and the others, but Nina insisted that Edward should stay with them; she enjoyed his company. The chartered plane left two hours before the family's private plane left. On the flight back, they reminisced about how this was one of the best trips they have had in years and how Martin and Daniel's girlfriends fit right in with the family. The flight was over twelve hours long, and each of them slept on and off. All of a sudden, they were awakened by the sudden violent shaking of the plane; they had hit a patch of turbulence, and everyone opened their eyes and looked around at each other. The pilot explained that he was going to move out of the air space and that it wouldn't last long; after a few minutes, the plane returned to smooth air space, and one by one they all started dosing off again. Nina said she remembered not being able to go back to sleep; she started to feel anxious and worried. She remembered getting up and going to the cockpit and asking the pilot where they were and how much longer they had before getting to San Francisco and the pilot disappointed her when he reported that the trip was not even halfway over. Nina said she has never really liked flying, but by then, they had flown so many times, she couldn't understand why she had reverted back to her uneasiness of the experience. The pilot assured her that they were on schedule and that it looked like the ride was going to be smooth from there. Nina said she remembered fidgeting; she tried to do a crossword puzzle, then she tried to watch a movie, but she couldn't concentrate. She said that Nick just opened his eyes slowly and began to rub her hand, then her put his arm around her and pulled her close to him. She figured Nick remembered the old days and how his calmness made her feel protected. He never said a word, he knew and just went into his routine of touching her gently, to help her calm down, and after about twenty minutes, Nina remembered the quiet. Nick had a way of making her feel safe, so she laid her head on his chest and just listened to the rhythm of his heartbeat; she could feel her body relax in the stillness, but her mind kept wondering why she was feeling so uncomfortable. Nina said she couldn't wait to land, and when they finally landed in San Francisco safely, she remembers thinking, "Thank God this flight is over."

When they landed in San Francisco Airport, the pilot announced to the family that his ground crew would get their things off the plane, and they were being asked to report to the US Customs office. Nick immediately responded by saying, "Yea, we know the routine, but we are not leaving our things on the plane." The pilot was very close to the family and had been flying Nick for years, even when his children were very little. He said in a calm voice there is someone in the Customs office asking for you all specifically, and they have asked me to inform all the passengers onboard this flight to come, to leave your bags and belongings onboard, and come to the US Customs office. Edward tried to keep everyone calm, so he said, "Well, what do they think, we have something or someone illegal on the plane?"

The pilot said, "I asked several times what this was about, and they wouldn't give me any information. They just told me to have all the passengers on board your flight to leave their belongings on the plane and an escort would be on the ground to meet you all." Nick Jr. became visibly irritated with the pilot and his lack of information, "What the hell is going on, and why do we need an escort?" Just then, Nick Jr. looked out of window of the plane and saw several uniformed sheriff officers waiting. The pilot said, "The escorts are supposed to be US air marshalls. I'm not sure what the sheriff is doing out there." Nick told them all, "Let's just find out what this is about. None of you have any illegal imports or drugs, right? If not, whatever this is about, we will be fine." Nina was the first person to get off the plane, and when she took her last step, she felt the same uneasiness she did while she was on the plane earlier. The lead sheriff held out his hand to help her with her steps. He asked if she was Mrs. ___ the wife of Mr. ___ and she said yes, then he asked if her husband was on the plane and she also answered yes. Nina said she just kept looking back, waiting for Nick to get off the plane. Nick Jr. immediately came up to the sheriff and asked, "What the hell is going on?" The sheriff asked him who he was. When he told him, he just said, "You are all being asked to come inside, and I will explain it when you get inside the US Customs office." After everyone got off the plane, Nina walked over to Nick and grabbed his hand. Nick asked the same question Nick Jr. asked, and the sheriff replied in the same way. The air marshall followed closely behind the family, with two other officers on the side of the family. When they all got to the door to enter, the sheriff turned around and said, "The area is filled with reporters, please just keep walking. You can even cover your faces if you like." At that point, Nick Jr. became unglued and started to talk very loud, insisting that someone tell them what this was about. The sheriff said, "I need to take you all inside, and I will tell you everything." Edward told Nick Jr. to just calm down. "We have done nothing wrong, remain calm." When the doors opened, there were so many lights and cameras, the two officers pushed the media and their cameras out of the way. The family had less than ten feet to walk to get into the US Customs office. A man of small stature walked up to Nick and addressed him by his last name, then the man stated, "None of you have done anything wrong." He held his head down and said, "I am so sorry, but our office was notified by the United States Embassy in Switzerland that the private plane chartered by you was in an accident. We were unsure who was on the plane, but the investigation revealed that it was going to be used for private purposes, and that your own private plane had the same scheduled flight plan." He hesitated and then continued, "It is with great sympathy that I inform you that there were no survivors."

Nina said she didn't hear anything else; it was as if someone had put the US custom's representative on "mute." She could see his lips moving, but she never heard anything else he said; she also felt like she had lost her voice. She could not believe the level of devastation that the man had placed on her and her family; all she could think of was her children, grandchildren, and the other family members that were on the plane. Nina said the room started to spin, and she became lightheaded. It was as if she had been hit by a high-speed train. She said she could feel her insides screaming, "My babies, my babies, my babies," but her screams were only internal because no outward sound was ever released. Nina knew she would never be the same again.

Nick and Nick Jr. were both simultaneously asking the man questions; he kept his eyes on Nick even though Nick Jr. was also standing there asking questions. Nick remembered Nina collapsing in a chair next to the door, but all he could do is look at her; he couldn't console her or even interact with her. He was in his own agony and needed more information to make sense out of what he had just been told. Finally, Nick asked the representative if the US Embassy knew if the plane and his family had been recovered. The room became still; it was the visual depiction of the calm before the storm. The man just looked at him and said there was nothing left of the plane and no possibilities of any survivors because the plane had hit a side of a mountain and exploded into flames. The US Customs office was full of sorrow, tears, confusion, and chaos. Nick just looked down on the floor and grabbed his chest; the thought was too much for anyone to bear. He went from feeling proud of his creation to responsible for their demise. He said he kept thinking, "Does he know who we are? This could not be happening to us. We are good people. We help those in need. We have never done anything to anyone." He remembers asking God, "Are we being punished for something? What have we done?" He agreed with Nina; in that moment, he knew his life was changed forever.

One of the family members asked how the media knew, and the man said he was not sure of the details, but the charter company may have released some of the information that the plane was chartered in the family's name, but they were not sure who the passengers were, so everything were speculations. He went on to say, "Our office has never confirmed or denied the accusation that your family in fact chartered the plane, nor who the passengers were, because until now, we were not completely sure who was on the plane, which is why we asked for you all by name on your private plane." Nick turned to Edward and said, "I wish it would have been me. I don't think I can live with this." Edward just put his arms around Nick and said, "We will get through this. God is a healer and a fixer." Nick said he was not ready for Edward to go into one of his God sermons; he wanted to say something disrespectful to Edward or asked why God had not fixed the plane from crashing, but he knew it was inappropriate, and it was not going to help him, so he just walked away.

Nick Jr. said, "We are going to need to notify Olivia and Alison's family, and Dana, Daniels first wife before any of them hear about it through the media." Caroline agreed to call Dana, while Nick Jr. tried to gather Olivia's family's information from his mother, but she never said a word. Nina just stared into space; no matter how many times Nick Jr. tried, she gave him no words, only sad eyes. Finally, Nick asked the sherriff if someone could do an in-person notification to Olivia's family; he told the sherriff, "I think it's going to be too much for them to hear over the phone. She was their only child." The sheriff agreed to have an officer dispatched to Olivia's parents' house to notify them of the tragedy. Caroline and Edward seemed to be the only ones of sound mind and body in the room. After Caroline spoke to Dana, she made arrangements for a car service to take them all home; she said Dana was going to meet them at the house. The pilot arranged to have everything that was on plane delivered to the house, and he accompanied their belongings. The sheriff told the family that they were arranging an escort through a nondisclosed exit so they could avoid the media.

Caroline announced that her daughters and Edward's wife and daughters were flying commercial and should be landing in the next thirty minutes. They wanted someone to meet them at the plane before they turned their phones on or get their luggage. Caroline asked if one of the officers could exhort her so she would meet them to join the family in the US Customs office and they could all use the car service and go home together. Nick Jr. told the first car service to take his parents and his sister Julianna and her husband to the house and they would follow shortly after their daughters and Edward's wife and daughters had landed. Nick insisted that they all stay together; he said, "We will all wait here for you to go and get them." He didn't want to separate, and he was adamant they were all staying together. There was order in all the things that transpired, even in the midst of what seemed chaotic. Nick couldn't remember all the details in order, but he remembered, somehow, they all got through it. Once the girls were notified and united with the family, they all left the airport and went to the family's home about an hour from San Francisco Airport. Caroline continued to take charge by contacting other family members; the house became crowed very quick. The media hovered outside of the family home, but the family was not ready to talk; they did issue a statement, requesting privacy and prayer through Edward's wife who was interviewed by a local reporter.

Nina's shock state worried Nick Jr. and Julianna, but Nick insisted that Nina was strong and that she would be all right, even though she only offered them a steady, blank stare. "She will be all right," he kept saying. The days to follow, many people tried to console Nina, but she was devastated and declined any visitors even her long-time childhood friend, Rachal, who had been through everything with Nina. Nina chose to reside in the comforts of her bed; she barely ate or spoke a word. Nick worked with Caroline to handle the memorial arrangements and information regarding the recovery of what was left of the crash. Nick suggested to the family that it would be too much to have seven separate memorial services, so they all agreed to just have one service. This required that they used a stadium to have the memorial service. The team that David had investments in arranged for the local stadium to be used; the date was set; family, friends, and employees of the family were all invited.

Olivia's family had a separate service that the whole family attended. Although the family had met Olivia on several occasions, they realized that they didn't really know her or her family until her memorial service. Many people got up and spoke about how kind and wonderful she was and how she had gone out of her way to help others. They talked about her volunteer work, her faith, her gift, and her relationship with God. Nina remembers thinking that Olivia was much like Martin, and she wished she had spent more time with her. She also realized why Martin loved Olivia so much and wanted her to go on the family vacation with them. Nick spoke on behalf of the family; he was grief-stricken. He told them that his family had really gotten to know Olivia on their family vacation, and she had been a special addition to the vacation. Nick recalls feeling so guilty watching Olivia's parents with their pain at her service; he couldn't look them in the eyes. He felt their hearts breaking with grief, and there was nothing he could say or do to encourage them because he didn't know what to say or do.

Nick remembers not sleeping for days leading up to the service of his own family members. He also remembers avoiding anyone that wanted to explain God's will or plan and how God didn't make mistakes. In fact, he believed that this was not only a mistake; it was one of God's biggest mistakes. How could he not have made a mistake; how could he allow such suffering for one family, for one man? Yes, God had defiantly made a mistake this time, and Nick didn't want to talk about it. He was angry, hurt, bitter, confused, and disappointed all at the same time. It was as if someone had taken over his body; he kept telling himself to just hold it together for two more days. He believed that after the service was over, he would get some relief and his anxious feelings would subside. He kept looking at his watch, and it felt like time was standing still; he went from counting down the days to counting down the hours until the service. Nick could feel the weight of his guilt, hurt, and anger in browed in a tug-of-war on his emotions, and he worried about everyone and everything involving the service. He also remembers worrying if his other family members were blaming him because he was blaming himself, which made it hard for him to talk to anyone, especially Nina. He couldn't even make small talk with anyone for long. The only conversation he could truly hold was about the planning details of the service. He kept himself extremely busy, making sure he took care of every detail concerning the services, while Nina didn't get involved at all. In fact, Nina didn't have a clue what day or time the service started. She waited for Nick's daily updates and just nodded. At one point, she reminded him that there were no bodies to have a funeral and wanted to know what was he working on. His only response was, "There is still a lot of details to the service. I just want to make sure we don't miss a step." Nick was unaware that he was keeping busy, trying to avoid as many people as he could, trying to avoid the moment and the feeling that went with the moment. He believed that if he just kept moving, he could avoid feeling the magnitude of his pain and others would not be able to see his hurt and guilt. He avoided eye contact and holding long conversations; he avoided his reality because if he dared to take in what had really happened, he knew he would not make to or through the service.

On the day of the memorial service, Nina was unable to get out of bed. Julianna asked her friend Rachal to tell her mom to get it together. She knew that her mom and Rachal were close and that usually when her mom had a problem, she always seemed better after her and Rachal had spent some time together. Nina recalls this being the most heart-wrenching day she had ever faced, and even though she had been avoiding Rachal, she really needed her and her friendship that day. Nina, remembers Rachal telling her that "God has a purpose for life and death, and even though it hurts really bad right now, eventually you will get through this rough time, you will get through it." She went on to say, "Those we love are the embodiment of our being and it's hard to imagine life without them. They will always be with you in your thoughts. Just think about the love, the good times, hold on to your memories, because you guys had a lot of good memories. They would want you to remember the love, even though it's painful right now, do it for them." Nina remembers thinking Rachal may have had good intentions, but she didn't have any idea about the amount of pain she was experiencing; she had lost her children, grandchildren, daughter-in-law, brother-in-law, and other family members. All that was left is memories; how could she think about good times at a time like this.

Nina also remembers being grateful that Rachal advised her how important it was to attend the funeral and say her final goodbyes to those she loved. She didn't know how she was going to get through it at the time; she kept thinking about her family and how scared they must have been during those last minutes. Nina said she remembers feeling overwhelmed and motionless at the same time during the service and what made it even worst was the fact that there were no physical bodies to look at or touch. She said it was all like a bad dream, and she kept asking God what had she or anyone in her family done to deserve such devastation, such indescribable amounts of pain; how could something like this happen to such good people?

There were thousands of people in attendance at the memorial service and many offered their condolences to the entire family. Some people knew them all, while others had individual relationships with each of them. The family's businesses were all closed for the day, and every employee was invited to attend if they wanted to, and all of them did just that. There were customers, friends, and other relatives in attendance. Martin, Ethan, and Andrew's school friends attended, while David and Daniel had personal and business associates that were in attendance. It was one of the largest memorial service ever held in the state. There were seven eulogies performed and a different person spoke about the life of each one of those being eulogized.

Julianna remembers friends, colleagues, and family members telling stories about each of them; it was an extremely emotional day. They laughed, cried, and then laughed and cried again. She described it as an "emotional gumbo" filled with sadness, love, anger, joy, hurt, fear, and on that particular day, "hope" was at the bottom of the pot, and every now and then, it would swell to the top by someone's thoughtful memory shared in a story or a small child's stare, as an adult wiped the tears from their eyes, or even the silence that filled the room during the transition of speakers was powerful. It was a loud silence, and she remembered thinking, "Hurry up and start talking again so she didn't have to feel the absences of those she lost and the presences of her pain and devastation." Julianna kept staring at her father; she had never seen him broken. He had always been a strong, powerful man, the provider, the protector, and the guardian of the family, but on this day, Nick needed someone else to take the lead. He was in need of being provided for and protected. The family had never experienced tragedy at that level; if the truth be told, not many families have or will ever experience tragedy at that level. Nick felt responsible for each one of those being eulogized that day; he carried the burden and belief that their deaths were his fault. He was filled with lots of "if only"; he believed he had the power to change fate and destiny—if only he had not chartered the plane, if only he had been on that plane, if only they had left a few hours later or earlier, so many if onlys that ran across his mind suggested he could have done something different and the outcome would have been different. Nick is not alone; we all second guess our choices and decision when we experience tragedy. We question ourselves, others, and even God about what could've, should've, or would've happened if we had made difference choices; but the truth is, we are not in control of the outcome or destiny of another person. We don't even have complete control of our destiny.

Grief can either paralyze you or send you into a high or over-functioning energetic doer. The person who is paralyzed by the experience of grief will look much like Nina and find most task difficult, barely able to do anything, including hold a conversation. On the other hand, the high or over-functioning griever will keep busy and have a "I'll take care of it, I'll handle it, I'll get it" responses to almost everything concerning their surroundings, including funeral arrangements. The grief posture of the over-functioner is an unconscious rejection of the grief experience; it's a cover-up to conceal the hurt and pain. Unattended grief was taking its toll on Nick, and even he knew he was in trouble, but he just kept moving, trying to ignore the level of devastation he was experiencing, staying busy helped him avoid spending time with his thoughts or his grief, but at some point, one must attend to the symptoms of grief, and Nick was getting to that point. Nick was the product of a privileged life, never had an unmet need; he always had things done for him and if he wanted something, he would just buy it and experience instant gratification! This experience with loss made Nick come face-to-face with several of life's truths for all human beings; no matter how much wealth you have, you can never buy more time or bring back yesterday. Nick knew he would never be able to afford what this experience had cost him. He also met the reality that we all must die, and no amount of money was going to exempt him or his family from that fate. Nick didn't know exactly what he needed, but he knew he needed something much more powerful than himself, he also knew that he would never be the same.

After the family left the services, each of them grieved differently. Nina slipped into a depression; she eventually had to be hospitalized for a few days and diagnosed with major depression. It was without question that the root cause of the depression was complications in the grieving process. When Nina was released, Nick worried about her and her sadness. He searched for something familiar in his existence and believed that things could get back to normal, whatever normal was. Nick remembers hearing someone say that as time passed, his daily routines would help create "a new normal." He finally returned to work and tried to conduct business as usual, but every day, his thoughts were consumed with grief and the impact the loss had on him and his family. Nina had slipped into full-blown major depression and barely said ten words in months. One day, Nick was going through a jacket pocket and came across a little pamphlet that someone had given to him months back. He couldn't even remember where he had got it or who had given it to him. He was in a hurry, so he took it out of his jacket pocket and shoved it in his pants pocket.

Nick said the days were starting to feel real long, which caused him to want to shut the days down early, so he started an unhealthy habit of self-medicating with a glass of whatever was on the bar at home; it varied from vodka to whiskey, it didn't really matter to him. He remembers it helped him to cope with what he called "the long day of suffering." On one particular day, he made a stop at the beverage store to replenish the bar and the clerk ask if he was having a party; at first Nick just said no, then he looked at everything in the basket. He felt embarrassed by the fact that he had brought enough liquor that he could have actually gave a party; on the other hand, he didn't really plan to drink it all, but he wanted to make sure that he didn't run out again. As Nick was paying for all of his nonparty liquor, he realized he didn't owe the clerk or anyone else an explanation about what or why he was buying anything. The clerk just needed to do his job, he thought. While Nick waited patiently for the clerk to bag the items, he stuck his hands in his pants pocket, and he felt the little pamphlet again; he had planned to read it or at least open it up; he knew he put it in his jacket pocket for some reason, and he was carrying it around and planned to find out what it said. Nick left the beverage store and decided he could at least buy some food to go with all the liquor, so his next stop was at his and Nina's favorite restaurant; everyone in the restaurant knew him and Nina. They had sent food to their house after the tragedy, and they kept checking in with family members to find out how they were doing. When the maître d' saw Nick, he became excited and welcomed him with a heartfelt hug; he asked how Nina and the rest of the family was doing. They talked for a few minutes. He told him that he was praying for him and his family. Nick thanked him and informed him that he wanted an order to-go. He told him, "I'll take care of it. Don't worry, I'll get your usual." While Nick waited, once again, he stuck his hand in his pocket and this time, he pulled out the little gold pamphlet that had been following him around all day and started to read it. The first thing he read was, "Have you heard of the Four Spiritual Laws?" Nick looked around the restaurant and answered to himself "no." He turned the page, and the next page stated, "Just as there are physical laws that govern the physical universe, so are there spiritual laws that govern your relationship with God. Law 1: God loves you and offers a wonderful plan for your life." Nick kept reading, he learned God's love, God's plan, man's sinful nature, how man is separated from God, His sacrifice, His death, and His resurrection. Nick kept reading and remembered thinking, "Was this really what you had planned for my life, God?" Nick had several cynical questions for God and his plan as he kept reading. He could see some of his characteristics in Law 2: "Man is sinful and separated from God. Therefore, he cannot know and experience God's love and plan for his life." What really stuck out for Nick was illustrated example in the diagram and man's failed efforts to reach God, through his own efforts. Law 3: "Jesus Christ is God's only provision for man's sin. Through Him you can know and experience God's love and plan for your life." By the time he got to Law 4, "We much individually receive Jesus Christ as Savior and Lord, then we can know and experience God's love and plan for our lives," Nick could feel the sadness. He wanted to know what he had done that God would allow him to have this devastating experience. He kept going over the fact that he was not like other businessmen; he helped those in need, he gave to the poor, in fact, more that 10 percent of his wealth was allocated to helping those less fortunate. Why, God, why? Nick started to feel overwhelmed and tears started to swell up in his eyes, and suddenly, one of the restaurant workers walked up and greeted him, "Long time no see," without looking at him. She looked down at the pamphlet and said, "Hey, I've read that. It changed my life. Nice to see I'm not alone. I carry mine around too. Please be sure to tell your wife hello. Tell her that I'm back and things are good." With a big smile, the clerk said, "Have a nice day, and yes, God does have a wonderful plan for your life and I'm living proof of that." Nick didn't say a word; he just remembered thinking, "Maybe I missed something," and he stuck the little pamphlet back in his pocket, pulled himself and his thoughts together, and waited for his food.

When Nick got home, he brought the bags of liquor and food and set them on the kitchen counter and went into the room where Nina was and informed her that he had picked up dinner from their favorite restaurant. Nick said he sat on the edge of the bed and just stared at Nina. How did we get here, God? Will we ever be the same again? Is this really your plan for us? Nick said they were just sad; no other way to explain it—sad and hopeless. Nick told Nina that all the workers at the restaurant asked about her and told her about the young lady who said to tell her hello and that she was back and doing good. Nina asked Nick her name, but Nick never caught her name, then Nina sat up in the bed and described her. Nick said, "That's her," then Nina said, "She's back, oh, that is so good to hear. She is the lady who lost her son three years ago. He was the one that was killed after he and some other kids were experiencing pleasure strangulation."

Nick said, "That was her. She looked too young to have a child that died. I didn't know that was her. I would have said something more to her. I bet she thinks I'm rude." She saw me reading this little pamphlet and said it changed her life. Nina asked what pamphlet, so Nick pulled it out of his pocket and handed it to Nina; she looked at it for a long time, and then started reading it. by the time she finished, she was crying so hard. Nick didn't know what to do. He had witnessed Nina cry many times before, but something was different about her reaction to reading the pamphlet. Nick asked her if she was all right. She said she had read that same pamphlet before she had met him, and she had the same reaction then. How could we neglect God after all he did for us. Nina said, "God has been talking to me for years about my relationship with him, but something always came first. I always put something before him. I just want to say I'm sorry. I would like to go and talk to the young lady at the restaurant. Maybe she can tell me how it changed her life. She was so devastated the last time I saw her at her son's funeral. I would love to see her." Nina had not left the house in four months, and all Nick was thinking was he would do anything to get Nina up and out of the house again; he was excited that Nina agreed to go to the restaurant and could hardly wait for the next day.

The next day, Nick left work early and went home to pick Nina up; he wasn't sure what to expect when he got home, but when he walked in the house, Nina was dressed and ready to go. He was glad to see her all fixed up. He thought to himself, "She is still beautiful," and he was glad to see his wife up and dressed. She looked at Nick and said, "Are you ready to go?" Nick smiled. "Ready when you are." He looked at her and said, "You really look nice." She thanked him, and they walked out of the house. When they got to the restaurant, Nina experienced the same pleasant greetings that Nick received the day before. It felt right; Nina smiled and asked if Youlanda was there. Her co-worker informed them that she was scheduled to be at work in twenty minutes. Nina said, "We will wait," then the waiter showed them to a seat and they waited. After about ten minutes, Youlanda came over to the table and greeted Nina and Nick with a hug. Nina asked her to sit down, and they started to talk. She asked Nina how she was doing and told her she couldn't imagine how she was feeling. She had lost only one child, and Nina had lost several family members including her child and grandchildren. Youlanda said she had been through some battles, including major depression and thoughts of suicide; it had been a long road. She told Nina she had joined a church that had a support group for mothers who had lost children, and she had met lots of supportive people at the church and in the group, which helped her in her storm. She looked a Nina and Nick and said, "It takes time, but with God and time, it will get better, I promise you." Nina and Nick both felt their eyes fill up with tears; too proud to let them drop, Nick excused himself for a minute and went to the men's room, while Nina allow the emotional moment to have its way. Nina grabbed some tissue off the table and stayed engaged in the conversation with Youlanda. She asked her to forgive her for the crying. Youlanda told her that was a healthy response. Nina told her that she really looked good and asked her how long she been back to work. Youlanda said it was time for her to clock in. Nina hugged her again and said, "I was wondering if you would like to get together sometime and just talk." Youlanda smiled hard and said, "I would love to." Youlanda was flattered that Nina wanted to get together and talk; she knew that they had very little in common. After all, Nick and Nina had enough wealth to not only own the restaurants she worked in, they could even own a chain of them. What Youlanda did know is they were oddly joined together and shared a common acquaintance named pain and suffering; she also knew how much it helped to sit and talk or cry or just quit and have someone understand the silence. She knew Nina and Nick were kind and caring people. Nina even came to her son's funeral three years prior and extended a generous contribution toward the service. They exchanged numbers, and Youlanda told Nina she would call her the next day, and Nick said his goodbyes and thanked her for talking to them. Nina said, "Talk to you tomorrow," and they parted ways.

Nick was so excited to see Nina making an effort to participate in life; it seemed to lift his spirits, and that day, he didn't even think about taking his routine nightcap that he had come to enjoy and depended on for the past few months. Nina and Nick talked all the way home about how good Youlanda looked and how positive she seemed. Nina was curious about the support group and if it was the reason she looked so good was because of it.

The next day, as promised, Youlanda and Nina got together at Nina's house for muffins and coffee. They talked and cried and talked and cried for hours. Youlanda told Nina that she had no hope until she met God on his terms. She explained that she and God had been acquaintances off and on while she was growing up, but they never made it to the friend's stage because she only called him when she was in trouble and when her son died was no different. She told Nina that she spent many months just being upset with God because she believed for what she believed. She said she became so depressed that she had to be hospitalized, and she just wanted to die; she even remembered praying to God to just let her die at one time. Nina and Youlanda talked for hours; Youlanda asked her what her relationship with God was like. Nina admitted that she and Nick did not go to church except on special occasions, weddings, Easter, and occasional invites from friends and families for special events. Nina went on to share that Nick's brother was one of the leaders in his church, but they have never made a connection in the church; it actually seemed boring to them and found it pretty hard to follow the rituals. Youlanda told Nina she had felt the same way about many churches in the past; it was mostly because people seem to know what was going on, and she felt lost in the service. Youlanda said one of her friend's sister invited her to the service; she also had suffered loss of a child and said that the church had several different support groups that met regularly. On Youlanda's first visit, she felt right at home; she made an instant connection with the people and the service. She said the members are committed to supporting one another with their time, talents, and resources and they are real friendly. She went on to say that she was impressed with the service; they have order, but it doesn't feel so ritualistic as the other churches she had attended in the past. If the spirit moves them in a slightly different direction, for example a need to pray about a death of someone, they will stop and pray for the person and family right then, or if someone has a testimony that will encourage the congregation, the pastor will allow that experience to be shared. They deal with life as it is happening, and they use God's word to help those that life is happening to. While Nina and Youlanda were talking, Nick walked in the house; he greeted both of the ladies and told them he brought them some food; he told Nina he tried calling her on her cell phone, but it went to voicemail, he assumed they were in deep conversation, so he didn't bother calling the house phone. Nick could tell they had been crying, but they still seemed upbeat. Youlanda jumped up and said she didn't realize how late it was; she said she had to facilitate a group. She told Nina that once a month, she was responsible for the support group at church, but the group met once a week, and they alternated who facilitated the group. She invited Nina and told her that the group had really helped her. Nina said she might be interested in attending the group the next week; they said their goodbyes and agreed to talk again. During the next few days, Nina and Youlanda talked on the phone off and on; they talked about healing, crying, and anything else that came up, until the day came that Nina attended the support group at the church the following week.

 After Nina attended the first group, she knew why Youlanda seemed to have so much hope and recovery from her loss. Nina told Nick that there were so many women in her group that had also suffered a significant loss of someone important to them that she realized she was not alone. She described them as being from every age, every race, and every social economic setting; no one is exempt from the experience of death. She also told Nick that the church had a similar group for men and suggested that he consider at least checking it out. Nick agreed after seeing how excited Nina was, and a few weeks later, he did just that. Nick also found the meeting beneficial and started attending the group regularly. After Nina and Nick attended several meetings, they also started visiting the church and eventually they decided to join the church that they had driven by so many times without a thought of what happens inside. Nick said one day he was getting dressed for what started off as another visit to the church, and he could feel the pull of the Holy Spirit on making a commitment on a regular basis to spend time with God and his people. Nick said he didn't say anything to Nina, but Nina kept asking him if he was all right that morning, and as they were driving to church, she asked him again. Then Nick said he turned to her and asked her if she thought God talked to her. Nina said God talks to her every day through his word. He asked her how she felt about joining the church, and tears started to form in her eyes, as she answered by saying, "I have been a member in my heart for weeks. I have just been waiting on you. God assured me that all I needed to do is be patient and that you were making a decision for yourself and your family." She grabbed his hand and smiled like she had not smiled in years. When the pastor of the church gave the invitation, as he had done for months, Nick and Nina both remained standing and accepted the invitation to become members of the local church that had exactly what they needed at the exact time they needed it. The pastor of the church was excited that they had made a decision that would change their lives forever; he had made the same appeal for months, but he didn't believe in pressuring anyone. He shared what God said in his word about fellowship, discipleship, and stewardship and left it to the Holy Spirit to do the work on those making a decision about membership. Nina said she didn't remember a lot about the sermon that day; she was anxiously waiting for the invitation to join church because she and Nick had already made the decision to join, and it really didn't matter what was being preached their minds were made up. Nina said it had been years since the death of those she loved, but not a day had passed that she didn't think about them. She found it hardest when a birthday was near, or the anniversary of the death, Christmas, or any other holiday because it just wasn't the same without her whole family. Nick and Nina are different people than before the accident, before the loss of so many people; they find some days harder than others, but they have learned to treasure every day and every life because they know it is a gift from God, without a promise of how long. God, their local church, and the members have become a part of their new normal; they have learned to treasure every day and every life they encounter as a gift from God. They know all too well that tomorrow is not promised and all they have is their right now, and love is the greatest of all the gifts from God.

Today, Nick leads the men's grief support group and he reports that weeping may endure for a night, but joy comes in the morning; just take it one morning at a time. Nina stated she knew she was going to die or be so depressed she would have looked dead, if she had not done something to respond to her sorrow and pain associated with the loss of her son and her other family members. She shared that joining a church that's founded on teaching the Bible saved her from herself and her pain. Nina is very active in her church and often joins the pastor in sitting down with families immediately after experiencing a tragic death. She said she rarely knows what to say, but God takes the wheel and gives her the right words at the right time. She said, "What a blessing that God would use me after I ignored him for all those years." God is a forgiving God; he knows we will question Him and His plan, but keep the faith, just as Job, the upright, God-fearing, blameless man who faced great loss and despair, the Lord allowed Job to experience worldly suffering, while developing his and everyone witnessing his despair spiritual faith and maturity in God. It is written that all that Job experienced, he "*did not sin nor did he blame God*" *(Job 1:22)*. Healing our emotional incarceration is in the word of God, he will help you get through our suffering. Just allow him to speak to you in his word. Nina and Nick know that they have to focus on the heavenly prize that God promises us. They know that no matter how much wealth, power, or privilege you have on earth, it is temporary and no one will ever defeat death.

Finding Peace

Years later, after the calls have long stopped, when everyone else seems to have forgotten the person who you have never stopped thinking about or missing for a moment, when it becomes rare that anyone even tells stories about him or her or even mentions their name, or how quickly the atmosphere shifts to blank stares or lowered heads when anyone close to the departed shares a memory or a story or just a mention of their name can change the mood in the room, you feel the loud silence in the room, as if it is taboo to mention the dead in a social setting, or that mourning or sad feelings attached to the person should have been resolved "by now." It's as if you can almost read their minds, "Wow, they still haven't moved on. It's been years," and even if no one in the room is thinking that, that's what you believe. You might be questioning yourself and wondering how long you will have your heavy heart or your sad feeling, or the loneliness that even in the midst of a room full of people you can't seem to rationalize. Well, once again, you are not alone; love is forever. Regardless of how long it has been, it's perfectly normal to never stop thinking about them and the life you once shared with them.

In Psalms 27:13–14, David offers us instructions on how to be fearless and trust in God, regardless of the circumstance, it reads, "*I would have despaired unless I had believed that I would see the goodness of the Lord in the land of the living. Wait for the Lord; Be strong and let your heart take courage; yes, wait for the Lord.*" Waiting while suffering is a difficult task for today's human experience because everything is instant, at your fingertips; humans even believe they can Google

God's answer for their right-now situation, but waiting on God helps us develop spiritually. We must learn to trust God's timing. David knew that God was bigger than his problems, so he focused on God to help him deal with his problems, and while he waited, he trusted God's will, God's timing, and God's way because David knew God was able no matter what the problem, and that is what God wants you and me to know. *He is able.* Are you ready? Charles H. Spurgeon says, "Wait at His door with prayer; wait at His foot with humility; wait at his table with service; wait at His window with expectancy." Problems should drive us to God, not away from God; even when they are accompanied by pain and suffering, just wait and depend on God and his promises. He will never abandon us! Our loved ones will die, we will suffer pain, but God will be with us past our loved one's lifetime, past our pain. His love is infinite, unconditional, and it will remain forever, beyond this physical life focus on forever.

God's power is present in your weakness. Read *2 Corinthians 12:9*. When your situation feels helpless or hopeless, God promises that he will "give strength to the weary and increases the power of the weak."

"Those who hope in the Lord will renew their strength. They will soar on wings like eagles; they will run and not grow weary, they will walk and not faint" (*Isaiah 40:29–31*). It may feel like none of this is possible right now, but put your hope in God, and he will guide you, even in the darkness, even when you are feeling unsure.

UNEXPECTED TURBULENCE

We live in a world that encourages independence, autonomy, and separation; in fact, we engrain it in children at a very early age. In Western society, children are taught that they must find their way so that one day that can act and think independently of their family of origin. Work hard, get an education, and the pathways to life will be relatively smooth. The world promises the "American dream" the "land of milk and honey" setting up a false sense of autonomy, which has the potential to create a "independent self-ideology" or a false sense that one has control over his or her own destiny, position in life, and even control over the world. It isn't until one has an unexpected experience or sudden loss is one's mortality or limitations questioned and answered with the reality that life can be unpredictable, and we lack control over the unavoidable turbulence that death brings in all our lives. Well then, if our experiences with unavoidable death are a part of life, why do the experiences of sudden death cause so much turbulence in our lives?

Christians are "set apart" and should be encourage to be dependent, of a collective mind, and to carefully consider their life choices and what the impact will be on others in the family, the community, the world. The Christian should never be singled-minded and think as if they are living for themselves and personal gain, at all times we represent the Kingdom of God to all those that are lost as well as our brothers and sisters in Christ. My sister and I have had many conversations on how to gauge our behavior, no matter what the situation we have agreed to behave in such a way, that we never embarrass God or the Kingdom of God.

Many people use nice clichés that could help us have conversations about how to react and respond to life's transitions, but the truth is, when the unexpected trials and tribulations happen, even the clichés can't help us see light in life's darkness. No one but God can turn that light on. The most prevalent cliché, which is always have a plan B and even a plan C, so when you are faced with life's un-expectancies you can defer to the backup plan for life, but the truth is, all you need is plan A for life; just defer to God's will for your life because with God on your side, his grace is sufficient and "God's plan A is a wonderful plan for your life." In my own life's journey, I have often used the cliché "use the hand you are dealt wisely," believing that in some situations, the deck was stacked against me as if life is a game that you can play to win or lose. It's easy to create a simplistic reality of the amount of control that we have over the circumstances we face and the outcomes of our experiences. I admit, choices have a cause and effect on the outcome of certain situations, but even freewill isn't free; it will cost you. Life is full of swift transitions, and we have to get to a point that we understand we have very little control over the outcomes of most of our situations or the cards that we are dealt, the plan is preset, predestined, prearranged; it's a fixed fight only God has that cause-and-effect control that will set you on the right path. Stay in God's will, and if you are unsure of God's will, just ask him and ask him for wisdom on how to handle the situations in his will; he gives wisdom generously. Max Lucado tells us that, "at the beginning of every act of faith there is a seed of fear."

Conclusion What's Left Over

Those of us who are Christians at times question our pain when we are impacted by the death of someone we love. We ask God why and how long. We ask God what we did or failed to do to experience this level of pain. The truth is, God has already told us that in this life, we will have trials and tribulations, but he also promised us that death is a part of life; in fact, he said we will only live once, but we must die twice as Christians. First, we die to our earthly selves and desires, then we experience a physical death at some point. Most of us have heard different cliché like see you on the other side, or rest in peace (RIP), which sounds like there is the possibility that after leaving earth, the person is at rest. If your loved one was a Christian, he or she is at peace, not likely they are resting; they are most likely worshipping in peace (WIP). No more working, no more sickness, no more stress; let's rejoice, they are with the Lord.

Respect the signs that explain "fasten your seat belt" because life has gotten bumpy. Many people have explained life as being a collection of seasons that are marked by good and bad, happy and sad, ups and downs, progressions and regressions, movements and stillness, and if you live long enough, you could find yourself cycling through these various seasons over and over again, much like the mark of time with the changes in weather; whatever the case, life will happen, ready or not.

Grief is in God's will for our life. "He will wipe away every tear from their eyes and death shall be no more, neither shall there be mourning, nor crying, nor pain any more for the former things have passed away." Revelation 21:4. Oftentimes, we have a hard time accepting that life and death are intertwined; they are an interconnected force that cannot be separated; they are just at different scopes of the life span and an end to a beginning. Everything that lives must die; everything that dies served a purpose.

About the Author

Dr. T. R. Anderson worked as a civil rights professional for the United States government for over thirty years, serving people who believed that had been discriminated against in the work place. She's currently a counseling psychologist with a desire to help hurting people who have experienced trauma that has caused them complications in their daily life functioning. She encourages others to choose their words wisely because life and death is in the power of the tongue. Dr. Anderson is one of God's children who is a member of Paradise Baptist Church in Oakland, California; she loves her biological and church family and has a contagious sense of humor, endeavoring to find joy in every situation.

Joy is not controlled by an emotion. Joy transcends personality and emotions. It's wrapped in hope, not the hope in people, but the hope in God, because people are reliably unpredictable.

CPSIA information can be obtained
at www.ICGtesting.com
Printed in the USA
LVHW02s0902251017
553709LV00014B/366/P